"…a true gift for any woman seeking inspiration, support and encouragement as she embraces her vocation and aims to serve God by serving her family."

—DANIELLE BEAN, author, *Mom to Mom, Day to Day: Advice and Support for Catholic Living*

"Kimberly Hahn provides Christian women with a treasure trove of insights for fulfilling our vocations as wives, mothers and homemakers. Every woman seeking to live her life in harmony with God's will should have this book in her library alongside her Bible and catechism."

—GAIL BUCKLEY, founder and director, Catholic Scripture Study International, www.cssprogram.net

"*Graced and Gifted* is both encouraging and challenging. It is rare in our current culture to be fortified in our vocation as wife and mother. Kimberly has not only unveiled the biblical beauty found in the vocation of wife and mother, but also presented a very practical approach to growing in holiness each day. The study questions create a holy desire to be transformed through God's grace into the woman that God the Father desires for each one of us. I am eager to share Kimberly's insightful study on being feminine women in the second millennium."

—MICHAELANN MARTIN, mother of eight and wife of Curtis Martin, president and founder of FOCUS, The Fellowship of Catholic University Students

GRACED AND GIFTED

GRACED
AND
GIFTED

BIBLICAL
WISDOM
FOR THE
HOMEMAKER'S
HEART

Kimberly Hahn

SERVANT
BOOKS

PUBLISHED BY ST. ANTHONY MESSENGER PRESS
CINCINNATI, OHIO

RESCRIPT

In accord with the *Code of Canon Law*, I hereby grant my permission to publish *Graced and Gifted: Biblical Wisdom for the Homemaker's Heart.*

Most Reverend R. Daniel Conlon
Bishop
Diocese of Steubenville
Steubenville, Ohio
June 19, 2008

The permission to publish is a declaration that a book or pamphlet is considered to be free from doctrinal or moral error. It is not implied that those who have granted the permission to publish agree with the contents, opinions or statements expressed.

Unless otherwise indicated, Scripture passages have been taken from the *Revised Standard Version of the Bible,* copyright © 1946, 1952, and 1971 the National Council of the Churches of Christ in the USA. Used by permission. All rights reserved.

Scripture passages noted *RSVCE* are from the *Revised Standard Version of the Bible, Catholic Edition,* copyright © 1946, 1952, 1957, 1965, and 1966 the National Council of the Churches of Christ in the USA.

Scripture passage noted *KJV* is from the *King James Version Bible,* copyright ©1973, Zondervan.

Scripture passage noted *JB* is from *The Jerusalem Bible: Reader's Edition,* copyright ©1968, Doubleday & Co.

Note: The editors of this volume have made minor changes in capitalization to some of the Scripture quotations herein. Please consult the original source for proper capitalization.

Quotes are taken from the English translation of the *Catechism of the Catholic Church* for the United States of America (indicated as *CCC*), 2nd ed. Copyright 1997 by United States Catholic Conference—Libreria Editrice Vaticana.

Cover design by Constance Wolfer
Cover image: Bartolome Esteban Murillo, The Holy Family.
Photo credit: Erich Lessing / Art Resource, NY
Book design by Jennifer Tibbits

Library of Congress Cataloging-in-Publication Data

Hahn, Kimberly.
  Graced and gifted : biblical wisdom for the homemaker's heart / Kimberly Hahn.
      p. cm. — (Life-nurturing love)
  Includes bibliographical references.
  ISBN 978-0-86716-891-4 (pbk. : alk. paper) 1. Housewives—Religious life. 2. Housewives—Biblical teaching. 3. Homemakers—Religious life. 4. Homemakers—Biblical teaching. 5. Home—Biblical teaching. 6. Mothers—Religious life. 7. Mothers—Biblical teaching. 8. Christian women—Religious life. 9. Bible. O.T. Proverbs XXXI, 10-31—Criticism, interpretation, etc. I. Title.
  BV4528.15.H34 2008
  248.8'435—dc22

                              2008019895

ISBN 978-0-86716-891-4
Copyright ©2008, Kimberly Hahn. All rights reserved.

Published by Servant Books, an imprint of St. Anthony Messenger Press.
28 W. Liberty St.
Cincinnati, OH 45202
www.ServantBooks.org

Printed in the United States of America.
Printed on acid-free paper.

  09 10 11 12 5 4 3 2

I dedicate this book to my sister Kari Harrington, with whom I have shared many late nights discussing her recommended reading on marriage and family life. She continues to be a wonderful example of a wife and mom, mother-in-law and grandmother.

Contents

Introduction

*L*ife-Nurturing Love is a series of twenty-four Bible studies on the vocation of marriage and family life. The description of a godly woman in Proverbs 31 provides a table of contents for a topical study using a wide range of Scripture.

The first set of six studies is called *Chosen and Cherished: Biblical Wisdom for Your Marriage*. We focus on the core relationship of a family—marriage. This second set of six studies centers on the tasks of making a house a home, a place of beauty and order, where the needs of our loved ones are met.

The vocation of marriage offers us a rich opportunity to use the many gifts God has given us—talents, time and treasure—to witness to the world about our Lord. He has lavished his love and grace on us. Then he calls us to be a channel of that love and grace to our loved ones.

Besides the practical lessons on homemaking, illustrated by the Proverbs 31 woman, we see correlations with the ordinary work of housework and the extraordinary grace available to us through the sacraments. In each of the following six sections, there are two chapters of biblical reflections on an area of homemaking followed by a chapter relating that area to one of the sacraments.

The sacraments are not what we do for God but what God does for us. They are the means by which the Holy Spirit makes up for what we lack and gives us all we need to be faithful. They do not make us saints, but they make it possible for us to become saints.

The parallels between our making a home and God's making a home in our hearts are part of God's beautiful design in marriage.

You may have seen these practical and spiritual lessons lived well by significant women in your family, including your mother or grandmothers. Have there been other women who have taken you under their wing and nurtured you as a wife and mom? Maybe no one has mentored you, but now you are discovering good friends who are a little further along in life who enjoy assisting you.

I would like to be one of those good friends who share recommended resources and words of encouragement. Take what is helpful; skip what does not interest or apply to you. Like every other homemaker, I am in the process of learning how to do my tasks well, and since the seasons of life continue to change, that is an ongoing process.

Discussion groups, an indispensable component to this study, enable women to assist one another, especially across generations, heart to heart. Women can share their hopes for change, their lived wisdom from experience, and their requests for prayer. More questions are included than can be covered (listed in back). The goal is to jump-start conversation, not complete a survey.

Let's continue to take steps toward greater stewardship of the grace available so that we make better use of the gifts God has given us. Truly we have been graced and gifted for a marvelous mission in life!

PART ONE

*She
works
with
willing
hands*

CHAPTER ONE

Priority Loving Leads to Priority Living

In the midst of a conversation with my mom about home decorating, time management and caring for loved ones, I asked, "Mom, what is the key to homemaking?" If anyone would know, it would be she.

"Relationships are at the heart of homemaking."

My mother's response surprised me. She did not recommend a resource or offer a list of principles by which she had managed a home so well for more than five decades. Instead she explained that the art of homemaking had less to do with the tasks done inside of a house and more to do with the persons who make a house a home.[1]

Persons, not tasks, create a dwelling place. The psalmist declares, "LORD, you have been our dwelling place / in all generations" (Psalm 90:1). The Lord himself *is* our dwelling; heaven is our eternal home because he dwells there.

We express our love for God and each family member through our attention to the details of life. We accomplish our homemaking tasks in service to the significant persons in our lives. Remember: It is God—not the devil—who is in the details! How can we contribute to the well-being of each family member in terms of his or her needs for food, clothing and shelter?

In the pages that follow, I share practical tips and biblical insights that have formed my vision of homemaking, including resources that provide more details than I can recount in this book. In addition I offer a brief reflection on one of the sacraments following each pair of chapters on a homemaking topic.

FRAMING THE HOUSE(WORK)

An elderly priest provided a struggling mother, Holly Pierlot, with a framework to help her remember her priorities. His suggestion was simple: use five words that begin with the letter *P* to recall priorities in order of importance: *Prayer* (relationship with God), *Person* (your personal needs), *Partner* (relationship to your spouse), *Parent* (relationship to your child) and *Provider* (tasks of homemaking).

In addition Holly examined parallels between family life and the complexity of convent life: How could such a diverse group of people live in harmony? Could a family imitate this?

In her book *A Mother's Rule of Life*, Holly explains that a "rule" develops when a group of men or women share a particular mission. The leader writes a rule to balance the community's mission with caring for those living in community in terms of prayer, physical work and leisure (like Saint Augustine and Saint Benedict). Once the rule is written, all community members vow obedience to it, so that they live a unified life (which is part of the process toward a community's canonical status).

Individuals have also developed their own rules to serve as a compass for direction and forward movement in how they live their spiritual life in the midst of ordinary life.[2] Your rule of life—your overall mission through your vocation—can become a plumb line by which you evaluate and develop a plan for living the priorities of your life. You author your plan, balancing the contemplative (prayer) and active aspects (tasks) of your vocation. Then you commit yourself to follow your plan of life each day, by the grace of God, knowing that you may need to adjust for temporary imbalances such as sick children, pregnancy challenges, or sleepless nights with a newborn. Keeping your overall rule of life in mind enables you to stay on track while adjusting to curves and bumps in the road of life.

Some form of accountability—your spouse, your spiritual director or like-minded friends—can help you stay on track so that your plan means more than New Year's resolutions. Perhaps you could meet with other women to share words of encouragement and to pray for greater faithfulness for the following week as each of you makes progress. It's a joy to know that even though your walk your own path, you do not walk alone.

Your rule of life can expand into a prayerful, proactive plan for daily living that helps you to live your priorities. It guides you in following Christ in your state in life, which can bring greater "order to your home and peace to your soul."[3]

Your Plan of Life for Prayer

The first priority is *Prayer*, which evokes your relationship with your heavenly Father. When Jesus summarized the law and the prophets, he quoted Deuteronomy 6:5: "You shall love the Lord your God with all your heart, and with all your soul, and with all your mind. This is the great and first commandment. And a second is like it, You shall love your neighbor as yourself. On these two commandments depend all the law and the prophets" (Matthew 22:37–40).

You need to cultivate love for God as your deepest love, so that you can love others well with God's grace and strength. You may have natural virtues, good habits and a kind nature, but you will not raise a godly family apart from God's grace.

You love the Lord with "all your heart." Jesus is your Savior and Lord; he is the one who has chosen you and cherishes you. He laid down his life to restore your relationship to your heavenly Father; you owe him everything.

You love the Lord with "all your soul" through your growth in virtue and your struggle against an inclination to sin. He provides the grace you need through spiritual direction and the sacraments. He strengthens your will so that you struggle against sloth while increasing your devotion to duty and faithful obedience to him.

You love the Lord with "all your mind" by renewing your mind through studying the faith; then your prayer and participation in the sacraments is enriched. Your growth in the knowledge of the faith is not extraneous to your role as wife and mother but at the heart of those roles. Not only can you set aside time for disciplined study and prayer, but you can also listen to talks while you exercise or clean.[4] You can memorize Scripture, so that you can meditate on it while you carpool, garden or sit at a soccer practice. How often do you hear spiritual reading recommended and lament that it may be twenty years before you will have time for it? Instead you can make time now, in small amounts, for reading the lives of saints or *music* spiritual reading—it is time spent loving God with your mind.

Prayer is the breath of the soul, "the life of the new heart," according to the *Catechism of the Catholic Church* (*CCC*, 2697). Individual prayer is not a luxury we try to fit into our packed schedules. It is a necessity! Whether or not our prayer can occur before our little ones' demands must be addressed—how *do* they sense I am trying to pray alone first thing in the morning?—we need to drink deeply from the well of God's presence in order to refresh others.

Family prayer helps too, but it cannot substitute for our one-on-one time with our heavenly Father. In the 1800s, Susannah Wesley, wife of a pastor and the mother of ten children, devised a way to get some prayer time alone: Her children knew that if she sat in the kitchen with her apron over her head, she was praying and was not to be disturbed. In the 1900s a pastor's wife with three small children found that if she secured the room with all exits locked, she could put the children out of the playpen and climb into it. There she could pray or read her Bible without being touched for a few moments each day.

When Saint Paul instructs believers, "Pray constantly" (1 Thessalonians 5:17), he is addressing ordinary Christians with active family lives. He does not expect them to devote hours to prayer; rather he wants them to permeate the day with prayer.

Loving God includes resting in his presence whether we are at home in prayer, before the Blessed Sacrament in adoration or at Mass. We share the concerns of our hearts and regain his peace-filled perspective. We remember who he is, who we are and why we are doing what we are doing. Each day we renew our consecration for the day, and then our works, joys and sufferings become an extension of our prayer. We pray and then we act. We become heavenly minded *so that* we are earthly good (unlike the saying that claims someone is so heavenly minded that he or she is *no* earthly good).

A PLAN OF LIFE INCLUDES THE PERSON YOU ARE

The second priority is *Person*, meaning you! To fulfill the second greatest commandment—according to Jesus, to love your neighbor as you love yourself—you must love yourself.

You and I are called to appreciate who we are as beloved children of the Most High and then reach beyond ourselves to care for others. Truly loving ourselves is not inherently selfish; it is the antidote to selfishness. We have to be a "self" that is loved in order to give our "self" to another.

God teaches us how to love all others, including ourselves; for "we love, because he first loved us" (1 John 4:19). He wants us to love ourselves as he loves us, to accept his acceptance of us. He lavishes his grace and forgiveness on us, and in response we are able to extend grace and forgiveness to our spouse, our children and others.

Genuine love of self does not incur pride but humility. As Saint Paul warns, "Do nothing from selfishness or conceit, but in humility count others better than yourselves" (Philippians 2:3).

So how do you love yourself? You love your entire person—intellect, will, emotions and body—as an integrated whole. Saint Paul asserts, "Do you not know that you are God's temple and that God's Spirit dwells in you?" (1 Corinthians 3:16). You are to glorify God in your body.

For your sake and for the sake of your family's well-being, you cannot neglect your health. Avoid both indulgence and neglect—it is not unspiritual to care for your body. Even Saint Francis of Assisi, toward the end of his life, recognized that his mortifications had been too hard on his body. As Saint Paul cautions, "For we must all appear before the judgment seat of Christ, so that each one may receive good or evil, according to what he has done in the body" (2 Corinthians 5:10).

You may recognize your need for food, sleep and exercise, but have you thought through how much of each you need? You may be in a season of life when you cannot improve your sleep or add exercise, but can you discuss with your spouse or another mother these unmet needs to see how you can have greater balance? For example, is it possible to hire a mother's helper to take the baby on a walk or play with the baby twice a week? Knowing you could nap might make a huge difference in your outlook.

In addition, what about the unique health concerns women have: PMS, menstrual cycles, pregnancy and menopause? When we understand what is happening in our bodies, we can respond more appropriately. We ought not excuse poor behavior nor suffer in silence as if hormone shifts are not affecting us. When I feel out of control of my emotions, the mental picture I have is of a baby who accidentally scratches herself unless someone puts socks on her hands—Lord, protect me from myself and from inadvertently harming others. My mother so aptly quipped, "You have to take care of you *so that* you can take care of them." As we care for our basic needs, we are more attuned to our loved ones' basic needs.

Emotional health includes growing in self-awareness and self-knowledge. What are your natural strengths and weaknesses, given your personality and temperament? How can greater self-understanding contribute to the well-being of your family? Are your emotional needs being met: to love, to be loved, to have a sense of belonging and to have good relationships within the family? Are you factoring in any current family dynamic (a new baby, a move, a wedding, unexpected bills or a new job) that requires you to adjust to physical or emotional stress?

How about mental health? Have you identified positive and negative influences from your family of origin? What do you want to incorporate into your family, and what do you not want to repeat? Since all family trees are connected to Adam's, all families experience dysfunction to a degree, though some dysfunction is more serious than others. It is not a matter of adding one more rosary or one more novena to make a problem go away—problems must be addressed. We want to grow in holiness *and* wholeness.

Sometimes we need help from family, friends or professionals. Spouses and other loved ones are not mind readers; they may not offer help unless we tell them our needs. Then we need to respond to their offers of help. Even Jesus accepted the help of Simon the Cyrene when the Roman guards forced

Simon to carry Jesus' cross for him. Jesus knew it would help Simon to help him. Who knows how the Lord will work in someone's life when we permit him or her to help us?

We may need counseling, medication or changes in our diet, sleep or activity level. Perhaps we need a special day set aside on a regular basis for rest, relaxation, contemplation and reading—a time for spiritual direction and an opportunity for Confession that helps us discern what suffering should be "offered up" and what needs the assistance of a doctor or a counselor. In addition, we benefit from hobbies, crafts, musical instruments and talent development as creative outlets for personal renewal. We can also try a number of examples of creativity in the home offered by Edith Schaeffer in *The Hidden Art of Homemaking* (Tyndale, 1971). When our reservoir is full, there is more to give.

IF MARRIED,
YOUR NEXT PRIORITY IS YOUR PARTNER

The third priority, *Partner*, refers to your relationship to your beloved. Your covenant partner is your greatest gift, after Christ and his spouse, the Church. This priority is not on the tasks you do for your spouse but the relationship you are nurturing with him. For as Saint Paul alerts us repeatedly in 1 Corinthians 13, any action without love amounts to nothing.

Recently I referred to one of my children as "my sweet love," to which another child responded, "I thought *I* was your sweet love. Am I your *sweetest* love?"

"All of you children are my sweet loves. But," I divulged, "Daddy is my sweetest love." My comment elicited groans along with big smiles.

Priority loving in the family means loving your spouse first, your children second. The love of husband and wife is the wellspring of love for the entire family. Though your children's needs may seem greater and more immediate, be careful not to allow their needs to consume the time and energy needed for your spouse. Besides, the greatest need of your children is to experience the love of their parents for each other. If you do not have money for a sitter *and* a date, how can you get time alone together? You can create possibilities for being together by rising a little earlier to share a cup of coffee, enjoying the moonlight on the back porch sipping iced tea or sitting on the sofa in front of the fire to share your day once the little ones are in bed.

In the vocation of marriage, you become the primary channel of grace for your spouse; in cooperation with grace, you assist each other on the path to heaven. You may not be in the same spiritual place as your spouse, but you can share your journey of faith and each grows with and through the other. Saint Rita of Cascia is a remarkable saint for anyone in this situation. Rather than rejecting her husband when he was drawn into sin through his family's pattern of vengeance, she felt empathy for his angst and acknowledged his pain, all the while calling him to holiness.

In marriage you model for your children the kind of compassionate care and sacrificial service you long for them to imitate.[5] Marriage is not a "matching gift" program—if you give, I'll give—but rather a total gift of self to the other. Even when you fail, you show your children how to forgive each other and restore peace in a relationship. Marriage is a school of love for you and for your children. You may not be a saint yet, but you want to be. And you want your children to join you on this path toward holiness.

You build on a foundation of faithfulness as you demonstrate love and respect, especially as you work on communication and conflict resolution. You cultivate a spirit of thankfulness, appreciating your differences as well as all you have in common with your spouse. For a fuller treatment of many aspects of marriage, see the companion volume in this series, *Chosen and Cherished: Biblical Wisdom for Your Marriage* (Servant, 2007).

IF YOU HAVE OFFSPRING, YOUR NEXT PRIORITY IS PARENTING

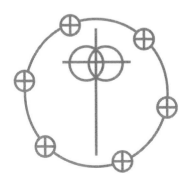

The fourth priority, *Parent*, refers to your relationship with each child, not just taking care of him or her. This relationship begins with receiving each child as a sign of your unity, a cherished and unique gift from the heart of your marital love and the heart of God. You and your husband have been made in the image and likeness of God. You reflect the self-donating love of the Trinity, a communion of life-giving Persons, as you generously cooperate in the creation of new life.

When you share your spiritual journey with your children, they not only witness your individual love for God but also your united love for him. You draw them closer to God as they follow your lead. More is caught from you than taught by you, though it is essential that you teach them about the Lord too. They share in the spirit of generosity: joy in new life, care for any who are sick, compassion toward those who are suffering and a sense of celebration for those who are rejoicing. It is in this spirit that the family functions as a domestic church.

As you share life with each child, you are aware not only of his or her basic needs but also of that child's dreams and aspirations for the future. You communicate better as you grow in understanding each child's temperament, personality, age and maturity—this is obviously an ongoing process. You nurture your children with love and discipline, with training and correction, forming them well, especially in the virtue of obedience. Over time you build a civilization of love and a culture of life in your family.[6]

YOU PROVIDE FOR THE NEEDS OF YOUR HOUSEHOLD

The fifth priority is your role as *Provider*. This is the focus of the remainder of this book and this set of six filmed studies: *You find your path to holiness in your state in life.* You do not finish homemaking tasks so that you can get to "holy" activities, but you find spiritual meaning even in manual labor.

Sirach 38:24–34 mentions a number of laborers who do not have leisure to study the Faith much but who are faithful to their tasks. The chapter concludes with this verse, "But they keep stable the fabric of the world, / and their prayer is in the practice of their trade" (Sirach 38:34). This applies in such a beautiful way to all labor, especially the tasks of homemaking. Ordinary work as an expression of prayer becomes extraordinary grace.

You love your family in myriad ways throughout the day (and night!). Many of the tasks do not seem very spiritual—taking out the trash, laundering, cooking, cleaning, earning a paycheck, carpooling, helping with homework—yet every task can have a spiritual dimension, provided you do it with great love. As Mother Teresa of Calcutta reminded us, "Prayer deepens faith and the fruit of faith is love and the fruit of love is service and the fruit of service is peace."[7]

You provide for the basic needs of your family as you clothe them, feed them and shelter them in a home that is both functional and beautiful. You want to be a good steward of the time, money and resources available to your family. In the midst of busy family life, you provide a nurturing atmosphere in which everyone can grow in holiness and wholeness.

PLAYING ON THE PERIPHERY—
BEYOND THE NUCLEAR FAMILY

Lesser priorities need a place in your Plan of Life. If you do not plan for them, they can dominate your schedule. They can become the tyranny of the urgent rather than the mission of the important. Or if you do not plan for these real but lesser priorities, you may find that commitments to your family consume you, leaving little time to reach beyond your household to care for others. So that you are neither dominated by nor neglectful of peripheral priorities, include them in your Plan.

What are the outer layers of the peripheral priorities of life?

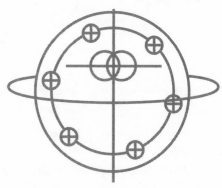

First, you have *Parents and extended family*—your parents, your siblings and their families and your grandparents, aunts, uncles, cousins and so on. And when you marry, you also become an integral part of each other's extended families. Nurturing those relationships takes a certain amount of time and thought, especially if you are to be sure your primary priorities remain primary.

Second, you reach out to those in your *Parish and neighborhood*—people who live close to you and share a common vision for creating a beautiful culture in which your children (and theirs) can thrive. This includes apostolates outside of your home as well as hospitality extended in your home.

Third, you provide leadership for *Public policies* that reflect godly morality. All law is an expression of morality; the critical question is, whose? Principles from the Church's social teachings can guide you. Through your work as a layperson who applies the Faith in the arena of ideas in public affairs, you can affect public policy for the good of all.

Fourth, you *Proclaim the Good News* about Jesus to the world. You can cultivate in yourself and your children a desire to evangelize the world for Christ by praying for countries around the world. You can support missions financially or with other resources, such as food, clothing, medical supplies and building materials. Perhaps you could even go on a mission trip as a family or send one of your children on a mission team. Share the Good News of Jesus with those who do not yet know him, while being faithful to the primary responsibilities of your state in life.

A Fresh Perspective From Your Plan of Life

Some days I plan a nice dinner, complete the laundry except for ironing and even pick up the first floor, but I have not had time for Scott or one-on-one time with the kids. Or maybe I get quality time with some family members only to realize at 5:30 PM that I have not even thought about dinner. No matter how much we achieve, it seems that we fail in some way every day. It can be overwhelming.

Does God intend for us to complete every homemaking task every day? No, it is not humanly possible. If it is not possible, then it is not God's will for us. Embracing the humility that comes from incomplete daily work is one of God's gifts to us through this calling.

Then what do we do when we feel defeated? We face our fears, failings and false notions about homemaking. We look at our tasks from a fresh perspective.

KEEPING THE BIG PICTURE IN PLAIN VIEW

When we approach each day with an overall Plan of Life, we become mission-minded rather than schedule-driven. The list of tasks may look the same, whether the starting point is the mission of our vocation or a schedule. However, the practical, physical work involved in the vocation of marriage is placed into the larger context of the shaping of souls and minds, changing our world for Christ. Now we approach each relationship, each task, responding to the Lord, "Yes, Lord, for you I will…" The tasks have not changed, but our approach has, as we keep the big picture in plain view.

CHAPTER TWO

Ordinary Work, Extraordinary Grace

"Keep your heart with all vigilance; / for from it flow the springs of life" (Proverbs 4:23). The springs of the life of grace flow through us so that we can accomplish our tasks with grace. Diligence over our hearts leads us to diligence in our tasks, the antidote to the deadly sin of sloth.

We have received many gifts over which we are to be good stewards: loved ones, food, clothing, shelter, land, time and resources. Just as David, a shepherd boy, learned obedience in small things before God called him to shepherd the people of Israel (see Psalm 78:70–72), so each day we have opportunities to learn obedience in small things, knowing that the reward of faithfulness is greater responsibility.

Jesus illustrates this point through a parable: A master left three servants of varying ability in charge of different sums of money while he traveled. When he returned, the master's response was the same to both of the servants who doubled the money, "Well done, good and faithful servant; you have been faithful over a little, I will set you over much; enter into the joy of your master" (Matthew 25:21, 23). However, to the servant who returned the money with no earnings, the master retrieved the money and condemned him as a wicked servant.

From this parable we understand several principles of stewardship. First, God calls us to work with what we have. Second, we should not compare ourselves to others—we trust that the

Lord has given us the grace and the gifts to do what he has asked us to do. Third, God expects faithfulness, which he rewards with greater responsibility; a job well done does not necessarily mean a job finished but perhaps cause for promotion.

What resources has God placed in your care? How can you grow as a steward of those resources? By God's grace you can and will grow in godliness so that he is honored by your efforts. And his reward will be to extend your responsibilities with greater gifts and the grace to be a faithful steward over those greater gifts.

THE PROVERBS 31 WOMAN

In Proverbs 31 we read about the stewardship of the woman of faith:

> Who can find a good wife?
> > She is far more precious than jewels.
> The heart of her husband trusts in her,
> > and he will have no lack of gain.
> She does him good, and not harm,
> > all the days of her life.
> She seeks wool and flax,
> > and works with willing hands. (Proverbs 31:10–13)

The Proverbs 31 woman cares for the practical needs of her household. She *seeks* things her family requires (though not necessarily everything they want).

In the remainder of this chapter, we will focus on providing clothing for our family. In the following chapter, we will examine how we are clothed in Christ through the sacrament of Baptism.

"SEEKS WOOL AND FLAX"

The Proverbs 31 woman *seeks wool and flax* because they are the best and least expensive materials for clothing. She uses them to make wool and linen cloth for any season. Thus she addresses her family's concern for clothing that is appropriate for the climate and meets their personal needs for attractiveness and comfort.

How do you care for the clothing needs of your family? You may purchase fabric and sew clothes; you may find better deals in department store sales or yard sales. Often families assist each other with hand-me-downs.

Care for clothing includes collecting, sorting, washing and drying your family's clothing in a timely fashion. Some people prefer to plow through many loads of laundry in a day; they have greater peace knowing that at the end of the day the task is done for the week. Others prefer laundering one or two loads each day; they have greater peace knowing that the laundry is not accumulating. Which strategy will fit best your Plan of Life? Your choice may make the difference between your peace of mind and always feeling behind with unfolded loads piled high on the Ping-Pong table!

What about ironing? Years ago I remember observing my mother-in-law's ironing pile, which included sheets and underwear. I could barely get shirts done! Fabric today requires less care than in years past, but some clothing cannot be worn with pride without ironing first. When I asked my mom how I could "redeem" ironing, a task I dreaded, she offered this thought: "When I iron, I pray for the person who will wear the garment—that their words and actions will honor the Lord." What a beautiful thought! Her encouragement has turned my ironing into prayer.

One of the greater challenges for women today is finding clothing that is modest and stylish. Given current fashion trends, how can we dress attractively without looking seductive? One way is to link with like-minded women to let stores know what will sell. An outstanding Web site that helps women do that is Pure Fashion, "a celebration of style and virtue."[1]

"WORKS WITH WILLING HANDS"

The fact that the Proverbs 31 woman *works*, rather than just assigns tasks to her handmaids, highlights the fact that labor is the duty of all. Physical work ennobles us.

Before sin entered creation, Adam and Eve had tasks in the Garden of Eden, so work is not a consequence of the Fall. However, their work became much more difficult due to the consequences of sin: Adam's labor to make the land fruitful now included thorns and sweat; Eve's labor to deliver the fruit of their love included greatly increased pain in delivery (see Genesis 3:16).

Diligent labor is constructive; sloth is destructuve. Proverbs relates how easily someone can slip into sloth, with major consequences:

> How long will you lie there, O sluggard?
>   When will you arise from your sleep?
> A little sleep, a little slumber,
>   a little folding of the hands to rest,
> and poverty will come upon you like a vagabond,
>   and want like an armed man. (Proverbs 6:9–11)

Sleep is a gift, unless it becomes an excuse not to work, for "he who is slack in his work / is a brother to him who destroys" (Proverbs 18:9).

Saint Paul charged the Thessalonians not to tolerate idleness:

> Now we command you, brethren, in the name of our Lord Jesus Christ, that you keep away from any brother who is walking in idleness and not in accord with the tradition that you received from us.... For we hear that some of you are walking in idleness, mere busybodies, not doing any work. Now such persons we command and exhort in the Lord Jesus Christ to do their work in quietness and to earn their own living. (2 Thessalonians 3:6, 11–12)

Saint Paul taught believers to work, and he gave them a good example. He expected them to continue working, even warning that anyone rejecting this teaching should be shunned, so that through shame the person would be restored to their fellowship.

Tabitha (also known as Dorcas) was a wonderful example of a woman who worked diligently with willing hands in the early Church. "She was full of good works and acts of charity" (Acts 9:36). Her heart of compassion for the widows in her seaside town of Joppa led her to use her rather inconspicuous, ordinary skill of sewing to bless them with beautiful clothes. She was equipped naturally for a supernatural work of mercy, to clothe the naked.

Many grieved when Tabitha died. Disciples preparing her for burial heard that Peter was nearby and sent two men to plead with him to see her. When Peter entered the room where Tabitha was lying, he was moved by the people's love for her and her obvious love for them, expressed in her handiwork. "All the widows stood beside him weeping, and showing coats and garments which Dorcas made while she was with them" (Acts 9:39). Her simple service had led to greatness.

Peter asked all to leave before he prayed. "Then turning to the body he said, 'Tabitha, rise.' And she opened her eyes, and when she saw Peter she sat up. And he gave her his hand and lifted her up. Then calling the saints and widows he presented her alive" (Acts 9:40–41).

What were the consequences of Tabitha's resurrection? First, word spread, and many people came to faith (see Acts 9:42). Second, Peter was able to strengthen the Church in Joppa, enjoying their hospitality until the Lord revealed the next phase of his mission: reaching out to gentiles (see Acts 9:43; 10). Third, Tabitha continued her diligent service for the Lord in sewing, willing to wait for heaven until the Lord no longer needed her service. Her simple deeds and heart of service produced a powerful witness.

"WORKS WITH *WILLING* HANDS"

The fact that the Proverbs 31 woman works with *willing* hands highlights her delight in her work. She has a cheerful rather than a complaining spirit about her work. The translation from Syriac says, "Her hands are active after the pleasure of her heart."

This is the attitude I want to have. Usually homemaking tasks do not frustrate me. Sure, doing the same chores week after week can get tedious, but I have been trained by my mother to see the spiritual side of things—it is possible to rise above the mundane to see the big picture. What seems like menial work can be meaningful work.

But one day I stopped in my tracks, midway up the stairs, with a basket full of clean clothes. There it was: the same Healthtex shirt I had laundered for years. Michael had worn it, Gabriel had worn it; Hannah had not worn it (since it was too boyish), but Jeremiah had worn it. Now, week after week, I was carrying it back up the stairs after Joseph had worn it, only to have him get it dirty again!

I was caught, for a moment, in the futility of what I was doing. The laundry basket almost became too heavy to carry. I cried out, "God help me! How many times am I going to wash this shirt? What's the point of all this repetitive work?" All of a sudden I felt caught on a point of self-pity, but I really *did* want a different perspective.

Almost immediately the thought came, *Think how many children you have been able to love, week after week, through this one little shirt.*

I paused. Though the task had not changed, I had. I realized, with gratitude, that though the work was repetitive, the work on my heart and mind was not. Through the mundane work of a homemaker, God was fashioning a home in my heart where love could be expressed in myriad acts of kindness, including laundering the same shirt, which has only recently been retired from active duty since David has outgrown it!

I was *not* caring for the shirt; I was caring *for the child* who wore the shirt. The load of laundry became light, and I carried it easily the rest of the way upstairs.

I realized that though I may be sweeping the same floor, wiping the same dishes, making the same bed, washing the same clothes, something is different—*I* am. Little by little God is giving me more of a servant heart as I relinquish my will to his, allowing the ordinary tasks of my day to reflect the extraordinary love he has for my loved ones through me. Through ordinary work God gives extraordinary grace. When I cooperate with that grace, I remember, "I can do all things in him [Christ] who strengthens me" (Philippians 4:13).

SMALL EFFORTS COUNT

Think about the little boy who gave Jesus all he had, though it was not much—just five loaves and two fish (see John 6:9–14). How could that gift even make a difference in feeding thousands? Jesus uses what we give him.

Another translation of "works with willing hands" is "makes cloth with skillful hands."[2] What are the skills we have in terms of clothing our family? Can someone teach us better methods of laundering, ironing, shopping (and keeping track of clothing sizes!) or sewing? How can we acquire more of the skills we need?

Hannah, wife of Elkanah, offers a wonderful example of clothing someone as an act of great love. She suffers years of infertility all the while enduring the boasts of Elkanah's other wife, who is very fertile. In her agony Hannah pours out her heart in prayer. She promises to give the child in service to the Lord if he blesses her with a son. Then Eli, the priest, tells her that the Lord will answer her prayer.

One year later Hannah and Elkanah are blessed with a son. Faithful to her promise, when Samuel is only three years old, Hannah and Elkanah bring Samuel to live permanently with Eli, to serve God for the rest of his life.

> Samuel was ministering before the LORD, a boy girded with a linen ephod. And his mother used to make for him a little robe and take it to him each year, when she went up with her husband to offer the yearly sacrifice. Then Eli would bless Elkanah and his wife, and say, "The LORD give you children by this woman for the loan which she lent to the LORD"; so then they would return to their home.
>
> And the LORD visited Hannah, and she conceived and bore three sons and two daughters. And the boy Samuel grew in the presence of the LORD. (1 Samuel 2:18–21)

Think of the loving care that Hannah put into each stitch in the special robe Samuel would wear for the next year. She could not be with him, but she could provide him a covering—each day he covered himself with the robe, he knew that her love and prayers covered him from a distance. And she worked diligently to make the new garment that he would anticipate her bringing to him the following year.

Hannah's tender care for Samuel is a beautiful image. We imitate her loving kindness as we provide for the clothing needs of each family member. We pray as she prayed, that as our family members are covered with clothing we provide, they will also be covered with a sense of our love and prayers.

CHAPTER THREE

A Mother's Guide to Baptism

Clothing is a covering. When Adam and Eve realize their nakedness, due to sin, they make a poor attempt to cover themselves with fig leaves and then hide from God. The Lord exposes their sin, giving them an opportunity to repent that they do not take. In the midst of pronouncing curses as consequences of their sin, he promises a Redeemer (see Genesis 3:15) who will cover their spiritual nakedness. Then the Lord provides the skins to clothe Adam and Eve (Genesis 3:21). As a good Father, he covers their nakedness.

One of the great privileges we have within marriage is to cooperate with God in the creation of new life. When he enables us to conceive and bear the child's body, he creates the child's soul. Then we have the privilege of bringing the child to Baptism, so that he or she is born of water and the Spirit.[1]

Just as we care for our children's need for clothing, so we make sure they are clothed in righteousness. In the baptismal rite "the white garment symbolizes that the person baptized has 'put on Christ,' has risen with Christ" (*CCC*, 1243, quoting Galatians 3:27, "For as many of you as were baptized into Christ have put on Christ"). What does it mean to "put on Christ"?

There is a popular misconception that to "put on Christ" is to be covered by Christ's righteousness, similar to snow covering a dunghill—Christ being the snow and we being the unchanged dunghill. The Catholic Church teaches that Baptism effects a fundamental change: God gives us the grace of his life, his righteousness, and restores to us the mystery of divine Sonship, so that we become "partakers of the divine nature" (2 Peter 1:4). Through Baptism our child is born of water and the Spirit (see John 3:5), and the Church is enriched with this new child of God.

Saint Peter declares, "You are a chosen race, a royal priesthood, a holy nation, God's own people, that you may declare the wonderful deeds of him who called you out of darkness into his marvelous light" (1 Peter 2:9). At the same time Saint Peter cautions that Baptism comes with a warning: You are now in a state of grace, but how will you live that grace? He gives a parallel between Noah and his family's salvation from the flood and Baptism:

> God's patience waited in the days of Noah, during the building of the ark, in which a few, that is, eight persons, were saved through water. *Baptism*, which corresponds to this, *now saves you*, not as a removal of dirt from the body but as an appeal to God for a clear conscience, through the resurrection of Jesus Christ. (1 Peter 3:20–21, italics added)

Eight persons were saved from the flood; but there is no proof that Ham, after sinning grievously against his father, ever returned to a life of faith (see Genesis 9:20–25). Likewise, Baptism places us in a state of grace, but we must respond to that grace or we can lose it.

I had an opportunity to explain this to one of my sons when he was six. As we drove he expressed his concern: "Mommy, I pray every day that I won't go to hell."

I did not want him to live in fear, so I decided to make a comparison that he could understand. "Son, do you think Daddy wants you to wake up saying, 'I hope I'm Scott Hahn's son, I hope I'm Scott Hahn's son'? Or does he want you to say, 'I *am* Scott Hahn's son. How can I act in a way that will please him?'"

I continued, "Through Baptism you *are* God's son. He wants you to waken each day, thankful you are his son, eager to please him."

That made sense to him. I needed to explain a little more. "Son, because you are our child, when we die, you and your siblings will get our money and stuff—it's called an inheritance."

His face brightened, "Cool!"

"Yes, except for the death part. But my point is that all we have belongs to God; as long as you are faithful to him, you will inherit from us. But if you abandon the Lord, we would have to take you out of our will, to honor God as good stewards. You cannot earn your inheritance, but you can forfeit it, if you are unfaithful. Likewise, you cannot earn your salvation—it is a gift from God, an inheritance; however, you can forfeit it if you are an unrepentant son of God. At the same time both your earthly father and your heavenly Father will want a restored relationship with you, so never be afraid to repent."

My son understood in a new way that he needed to delight in being a son of God and to confirm the grace of being a son of God by living in a way that pleased the Lord.

Baptism is not fire insurance from hell. It does place your child in a state of grace, but he or she must respond to that grace, or the grace of salvation can be lost. We assist our children in responding as we teach them the Faith, pray with and for them, celebrate the sacraments alongside them and give them the best example we can of a life of virtue and faithfulness.

Part Two

*She
brings
her food
from
afar*

CHAPTER FOUR

She Provides Food for Her Household

G od gives us food to sustain our lives and to bless us. After God created Adam and Eve, he blessed their union and offered them food: "Behold, I have given you every plant yielding seed which is upon the face of all the earth, and every tree with seed in its fruit; you shall have them for food" (Genesis 1:29). Following the flood God specified that animals as well as plants could be eaten: "Every moving thing that lives shall be food for you; and as I gave you the green plants, I give you everything" (Genesis 9:3).

The Proverbs 31 woman provides food for those in her care. "She is like the ships of the merchant, / she brings her food from afar. / She rises while it is yet night / and provides food for her household / and tasks for her maidens" (Proverbs 31:14–15). Her attitude is a combination of trusting in the Lord to provide coupled with her own hard work (see Psalm 145:15).

In the Sermon on the Mount, Jesus highlights the necessity of trusting in God's fatherly care for the basic needs of life—food and clothing:

> Therefore I tell you, do not be anxious about your life, what you shall eat or what you shall drink, nor about your body, what you shall put on. Is not life more than food, and the body more than clothing? Look at the birds of the air: they neither sow nor reap nor gather into barns, and yet your heavenly Father feeds them. Are you not of more

value than they?...Therefore do not be anxious, saying, "What shall we eat?" or "What shall we drink?" or "What shall we wear?" For the Gentiles seek all these things; and your heavenly Father knows that you need them all. (Matthew 6:25–26, 31–32)

Jesus acknowledges that concern is proper but anxiety is sinful.

The godly woman trusts the Lord to provide, and she works with willing hands to prepare food for her household. In due season, like the ant, she prepares for food that she will harvest at the right time. "Go to the ant, O sluggard; / consider her ways, and be wise. / Without having any chief, / officer or ruler, / she prepares her food in summer, / and gathers her sustenance in harvest" (Proverbs 6:6–8). She does not fear the future because she is ready.

SHE GATHERS FOOD

By planning ahead, the Proverbs 31 woman sets the atmosphere of her home. When others waken, they discover her preparations for their meal. Like the ships that bring food from afar, it takes time and a plan to provide good food; *not* planning takes more time and energy.

Like the ships we import a greater variety of foods than any king or queen could have required in past centuries. The selection we have at our local grocery store, in season or out of season, is plentiful. We learn the tastes our family enjoys, the nutritional value of various foods and the seasons that make certain purchases affordable. It takes time, but we can provide our family with a variety of colors, flavors and textures in the foods we use. Our thoughtfulness to detail is a blessing. "The plans of the diligent lead surely to abundance, / but every one who is hasty comes only to want" (Proverbs 21:5).

We may also gather food from our garden, vineyard or orchard. We have the satisfaction of working diligently and then enjoying (literally) the fruits of our labors, such as home-grown herbs, vegetables and fruit from berry bushes and fruit trees. "The soul of the sluggard craves, and gets nothing, / while the soul of the diligent is richly supplied" (Proverbs 13:4).

The possibilities inspire an enterprising spirit in us. We look for advantageous purchases as we hunt for bargains and use coupons. We gain practical wisdom from good books that show us how to stretch our dollars when it comes to food, such as *Miserly Moms: Living on One Income in a Two-Income Economy*. We may join food cooperatives, where people pool resources for better discounts on bulk items (but we do have to weigh the value of time and energy contributed to a co-op). We may exchange homemade breads, cookie trays or canned vegetables with friends, saving us time, money or both.

COMFORT FOODS

Nursing provides the original comfort food—breast milk—combining love with good-tasting nutrition. Often a young child receives solace from nursing, not only when he or she is hungry but also when he or she is hurt, sad, overtired or feeling sick. To bring comfort means to come and fortify someone. Jesus referred to the Holy Spirit as the Comforter he would send to the disciples, to be with them and to strengthen them once he returned to the Father (see John 14:16–17).

Comfort foods are tastes we associate with loving care, kindness, thoughtfulness and delicious flavor. They give us a sense of well-being. They can even open the way to a man's heart, for "a wife's charm delights her husband, / and her skill puts fat on his bones" (Sirach 26:13).

HOMEMADE IS WONDERFUL

What is important is not how expensive the food is but how much care the meal communicates. Wealthier people may be able to zip through fast-food restaurants more often than poorer folk, but it can be a cheapened meal. Occasionally drive-through food helps us, but is it frequent? We need to value the comforts of home.

As a wedding shower gift to her children, my dear friend Margo created her own cookbook, a collection of family favorites, crediting whatever family member had shared the recipe. Now she makes copies available to grandchildren and friends. She has deepened her connection with her children and their children as they share family traditions associated with food.

Another friend, Margaret, mother of ten and grand-mother of seventy (and counting), wanted to encourage her adult children's families who lived nearby. She visited their homes a few times a week, leaving some freshly baked goody in the kitchen—something everyone enjoyed and the young mother did not have the time or energy to make. Margaret did not require fanfare; she just saw an opportunity to serve and she did so.

Ethnic foods are a way that we can help our family con-nect the present with the past, either our heritage or our spouse's. We only had one ethnic food growing up in the Kirk family: German pancakes. We served them on birthdays (usu-ally with strawberries), on vacations (with piles of blackberries, raspberries, boysenberries or whatever berries we had just picked) and on other very special days like graduations, wed-dings and anniversaries.

When I asked Mom for the recipe so that I could make German pancakes in my home, she told me to look up "crepes" in the cookbook. What?! German pancakes are really French crepes? I am sorry, but my German great-grandmother made German pancakes, *not* French crepes (though I admit I use the recipe).

"Let nothing be wasted" is a motto I adopted from Sarah Edwards, wife of a famous eighteenth-century American theologian named Jonathan Edwards. It refers to Jesus' command regarding leftovers from the miracle of the loaves and fishes, "Gather the fragments left over, so that nothing will be wasted" (John 6:12, *NAB*). Even leftovers can be reused creatively, whether they are food, fabric or craft materials.

There can, however, be a limit to how many ways food leftovers can be used, according to one family. A dear friend on vacation with her family in Canada had been duly warned by her sons that the reheated meat was not to be served to them another time or they would toss her into the lake. She thought she was clever enough to put it into a meatloaf without their noticing. Needless to say, that night she went swimming!

She Prepares the Food

Late afternoon is low ebb for everyone in the family, including Mom. To avoid having hungry people hunt for you, grumble at you or snarf snacks from the cupboards, let them know you are preparing the meal you have planned. It calms everyone to know that dinner is on the way. When my mom was a newlywed, a friend gave her helpful advice: Thaw dinner in the morning, so that the decision is made for the day.

How about establishing a rotating menu in conjunction with the overall plan for the week, adjusting for sports schedules, errand day and Mass schedules? This simplifies the thought process involved in meal preparation; it may simplify shopping too. You can adjust the plan for a spontaneous meal out, a craving for pizza or extra leftovers you need to serve before they become science projects.

We can request a food list for each aisle at the grocery store or create one. Then we go through the sales flyer and know how to list foods for eager young helpers to find easily. We can also note any difficult-to-find items for future reference, as long as the manager does not get the idea of rearranging the entire store.

We keep a magnetized notepad on the fridge for listing missing or used-up items, unusual products needed for a new recipe or a food item for an upcoming event. We grab this list as we leave for the store, along with our list of sales items.

You can be creative with cooking. How about trying one new recipe each week? Perhaps you could double a recipe, freezing half for another time. Or you can adjust a recipe that serves eight for the exact number of people you will serve, like five or seven, using the Web site Allrecipes.[1] Even a change of location for your meal can add creativity, like packing a snack for the pool or a picnic for the park or a tailgate party.

The change of seasons can inspire an altered menu. The cooler weather of fall and the cold of winter, for those of us living in northern climates, remind us to warm the Crock-Pot for soups and stews and heavier meals like meatloaf and chili. Warmer weather in spring and the heat of summer nudge us to fix lighter fare, like special salads, and to fire the grill, especially when we would rather not heat up the kitchen while we air-condition it.

We also use creativity when we adjust the menu for the liturgical rhythm of life—times for fasting and times for feasting. We bring the Church's calendar into our homes in a kind of domestic liturgy, especially through mealtime. Two excellent resources for ideas on how to do this are *The Catholic Parent Book of Feasts: Celebrating the Church Year With Your Family*, by Michaelann Martin, Carol Puccio and Zoe Romanowsky (Our Sunday Visitor, 1999), and *A Continual Feast: A Cookbook to Celebrate the Joys of Family and Faith throughout the Christian Year*, by Evelyn Birge Vitz (Ignatius, 1991). Is there a way, through our meals, we can reflect the penitential seasons of Advent and Lent? How are we feasting in the Christmas season or the octave of Easter? Can we celebrate the anniversaries of sacraments for family members or their patron saints' feast days?

We can learn a lot from other families, provided we avoid comparisons that make us feel like failures. Perhaps we can incorporate one new idea into our family life or try one new recipe for a meatless Friday meal. When we share ideas and recipes with other families, we need to remember that we do not have to do everything, and we do not want to overwhelm anyone else. We thank God for the grace to do what we can.

WE COOK WITH A RIGHT ATTITUDE

Your attitude is as important as what you cook. "The fruit of the Spirit is love, joy, peace, patience, kindness, goodness, faithfulness, gentleness, self-control; against such there is no law" (Galatians 5:22–23). How can you exemplify this attitude as you prepare the meal?

You reveal "goodness" when you take time and give attention to detail. Let your prayer be, "Lord, help me to bless my family with this meal."

You model "patience" and "kindness" in the midst of interruptions while you cook. In this you have the opportunity to show mercy.

You demonstrate "self-control" by making a meal plan, following that plan and not snacking too much while you prepare the meal. However, 1 Timothy 5:18 cautions, "You shall not muzzle an ox when it is treading out the grain." Our family translates this as, "Cooks (and carvers) are allowed to nibble as they help!"

You contribute to "peace" by being prepared—you have a game plan and your family knows it. Hungry little children are willing to wait for fifteen more minutes if they know something wonderful is being prepared.

You show your "faithfulness" by providing good food, day after day.

And your efforts demonstrate your "love" shared with good taste and "joy"!

THE BLESSING OF GOOD SMELLS

Even a smell can remind you of a special time with loved ones. Certain smells trigger happy memories of various holidays— Thanksgiving, Christmas and Easter.

Many women bake bread regularly. When the smell of fresh bread wafts down the hall, hungry tummies are drawn into the kitchen. My mother-in-law's sticky buns are better than any restaurant's, and before we sit for dinner, we anticipate getting two each.

I have many memories of walking into our home after church on Sunday greeted by the smell of a roast, potatoes and carrots. Mom found a way to prepare a meal she could easily expand to include unexpected guests.

For the first twenty years of marriage, we wanted to simplify the process of Sunday meals to minimize the work involved. We used paper products and had a cold meal of sandwiches, fresh fruit and vegetables, chips, cottage cheese and dessert—a kind of indoor picnic. It was easy to expand the number of our guests with such simple fare, and everyone pitched in to simplify setup and cleanup. However, it was not the Sunday meal I remembered from my childhood.

After twenty years I asked Scott if we could change our format. I realized that we never used our good china (most of which had been wedding gifts), our good silver or even the dining room. Our children were getting older, and I wanted them to know how to eat in a more formal setting. I also had a vision of coming back from the Feast of the Eucharist each Sunday and wanting to reflect that in our family feast.

As we switched from the hearth to the dining room, and from paper plates and cups to china, silver and crystal, I noticed some changes: We lingered longer in conversation and laughter; we recorded a good thing of the week (which is becoming a precious treasure); and we enjoyed the beautiful setting that contributed to an overall sense of well-being. I am grateful for the change.

COOKING WITH CHILDREN

Many books offer creative suggestions for children helping adults create fun foods for the family. They range from nutritious snacks to full-scale meals. The library is a good resource for trying a recipe book before purchasing it.

A grandmother I know, Margo, has a different grandchild over each week. Baking is one of the activities they share. After dinner the child takes home a dessert to enjoy with his or her family. It is an opportunity to bond together and to bless others.

My sister Kari shared what proved to be a life-changing book with me: Mimi Wilson and Mary Beth Lagerborg's *Once-a-Month Cooking: a Proven System for Spending Less Time in the Kitchen and Enjoying Delicious, Homemade Meals Every Day* (St. Martin's, 2007).[2] Following their system, my sister had prepared and frozen a month's worth of meals. It sounded too good to be true, but I purchased the book and tried it. It was amazing!

I invited college women who thought it would be fun to cook for a day, and with the help of my children, we tackled cooking, chopping, measuring and bagging in gallon-size freezer bags about a hundred meals that would serve between eight and twelve people. I prefer once-a-season meal preparation more than once-a-month. If you do not have access to college students, it could be worth hiring some high school students for a day to watch little ones and help you cook.

The concept is great: You can minimize time spent in preparation and cleanup while you maximize available meal options by quadrupling recipes. For instance, it does not take much more time to make four meatloaves than one. Just line up the bowls, add the ingredients to each bowl, mix each bowl, fill a one-gallon bag from each bowl and store bags flat in the freezer. Most recipes can be frozen in freezer bags rather than in pans, so they take a minimum of storage space in a freezer. Some meals you cook ahead of time; some you freeze uncooked but fully prepared.

By having one mega-cooking day, you can simplify the process of food preparation in several ways. First, choosing from a variety of meals is easy because you have many choices available. Keep an updated list of frozen meals, so you know what options you have. Second, hospitality is easy because you know how many people you can feed with each meal. Third, helping people who need a meal—they just moved in, had a baby, have someone in the hospital—is easy. Just thaw two meals instead of one, and cook them at the same time.

Once you quadruple supplies for your favorite recipes, keep that list for future shopping. If you know you will need twenty pounds of hamburger and forty chicken breasts for cooking day, look for sales near that time and purchase the meat in bulk.

One time my sister Kari and some friends made an offer to an expectant mother: If you pay for the groceries, we will do the shopping and cooking, leaving you thirty meals in your freezer by lunchtime. The mother was delighted to have the help, and the moms offered a great gift of their time. When the baby arrived, the mom was able to combine meals offered with those in her freezer for about six weeks of help.

ABIGAIL'S HOSPITALITY IN 1 SAMUEL 25:1–42
Samuel, the last of the judges in Israel, who was also a priest and a prophet, anointed Saul as the first king of Israel. After King Saul committed two serious acts of disobedience, Samuel prophesied that the kingdom would be torn from

him. Then Samuel left King Saul and anointed David as the second king of Israel.

After David defeated the giant Goliath, he became Saul's armor bearer. His musical ability and spiritual sensitivity calmed King Saul when he was tormented by an evil spirit. The king even gave his daughter Michal to David as his wife. However, King Saul couldn't tolerate the praise his people offered David; he was overtaken by jealousy and envy. Let's examine the story as it unfolds.

David flees for his life from King Saul, escaping into the wilderness with six hundred men. King Saul gives away David's wife to another man. David seems to have lost everything.

While David is on the run, hiding from King Saul, he and his men provide protection for Nabal's flocks being kept in the wilderness (see 1 Samuel 25:15–16). Nabal, a kinsman from Hebron, near David's hometown of Bethlehem, is extremely rich and extremely rude. He is bad-tempered and self-centered. When David sends a request for provisions to be made for an upcoming feast day for him and his men—a just wage for his labors—Nabal makes David's messenger wait for his response. Then Nabal lies, saying he does not know David and perhaps he is really a runaway slave. David's response is quick: He and his men gird their loins with swords, intending to slay Nabal and all the men in his household.

Abigail, Nabal's wife, is beautiful, intelligent and wise (see 1 Samuel 25:14–22). She knows that David's request is just and that Nabal's lie has endangered the entire household. She knows what Nabal refuses to acknowledge—that David is the Lord's anointed, the future king of Israel. Though Nabal is unapproachable, Abigail humbly listens to his servants.

She knows that David's request is neither too difficult nor too cumbersome for Nabal. She acts quickly to save lives: She gathers enough bread, meat, fig cakes, clusters of raisins and jugs of wine to feed six hundred hungry men. Given a lack of refrigeration, it is astounding that Abigail produces a feast of this magnitude on such short notice. She acts on behalf of her husband without telling him. She will face his anger later, but for now she knows she should seek to preserve life, protecting the king from the sin of killing innocent people.

Abigail sends the food ahead of her. First Samuel 25:23–31 records the encounter between Abigail and David. First, she is gracious: She quickly dismounts, humbles herself, bowing low before David, and asks to take the blame for her husband, who is a "fool." If she had known of David's request, she would have acted. Second, she reminds David that the Lord has saved him from the sin of revenge; she urges him to let God act. This helps him regain his perspective, to see that day in light of the future.

Abigail then gives David food. She asks forgiveness for her husband; she intercedes on behalf of her household. She acknowledges that God has made him king and the trials he is experiencing will end. Her only request is for him to remember her when God blesses him, for she knows that God will in fact bless him.

David praises the Lord for this turn of events (see 1 Samuel 25:32–35). He blesses Abigail, grateful for her discretion. Her good sense has kept him from sin. Though David's killing the men would have freed her from her wretched husband, her compassion extends to the whole household. David accepts her gift, hearkens to her voice and grants her petition to save her people.

When Abigail returns home, Nabal is eating like a king, though he has denied the true king bread he has earned (see 1 Samuel 25:36–38). He is so drunk that he is unable to talk with her, so she waits until the morning when he is sober. Abigail tells Nabal everything, and he has a stroke. Ten days later Nabal dies.

When David hears of Nabal's death, he realizes a number of truths (1 Samuel 25:39–42): First, God has preserved him from sin and defeated his enemy without any blood-guilt. Second, Abigail's service of food for the king was for the love of God and to preserve life. Third, though Nabal refused David a small amount of food in payment, now all of Nabal's possessions will become David's. Fourth, Abigail's character has been revealed to David, and now she is free of her husband.

When Abigail responds to David's request to come to him, she is willing to be his handmaid, but he asks her to become his wife. She did what was right without knowing that she would become his queen! Moral of the story: We never know what will result from a gift of food.

SHE SERVES THE FOOD—
GRACIOUS LIVING IN THE DINING ROOM

The dining room is the second most important room in the house for family life. If you ask any of my siblings, they will tell you that the dining room is their favorite room in the house in which we were raised, partly due to delicious food but also due to the beauty of the table and meaningful conversations we had there.

When it comes to table setting, think through the details and see the possibilities. Try not to feel paralyzed if you do not know where to begin or feel as if you cannot always set an attractive table. What is something you can do to contribute to the meal in terms of beauty?

We can decorate the table with candles or flowers. My friend Deb mixes some store-bought flowers with small branches of leaves from the yard to make simple, attractive arrangements for the table. Tablecloths or placemats can be purchased inexpensively from yard sales or the dollar store. A tablecloth with a print will help hide small spills. Over time it is possible to acquire tablecloths to match the major liturgical colors for use on Sundays. Perhaps you could add these to your wish list for Christmas or ask your mother or mother-in-law if they have tablecloths they would be willing to give you. You can add a dimmer to the light switch for ambiance.

We all need beauty. Consider including a flower on a tray of food for someone who is sick or when serving Meals on Wheels to an elderly person. In Japan the presentation of the food is almost as important as the taste. Can we take an extra moment to use pretty serving bowls for the vegetable rather than the microwaveable bowl in which we bought it, or to put drinks into pitchers rather than placing cartons on the table, or to place condiments in small containers rather than having bottles of condiments on the table? The plastic containers are not bad or wrong; it's just that dishes make a nicer setting.

Place cards are simple additions for special holidays, birthday or anniversary parties, rehearsal dinners or wedding receptions. They communicate, "I prepared for you. Welcome!" You enable better conversation because of the placement of people, and you remove the awkwardness of people not knowing where to sit.

Family meals have become few and far between for many American families. If we want a family meal, we have to plan it around work schedules, sports practices or games, music or play rehearsals and a host of activities such as choir, Scouts and youth group. All of these activities can be worthwhile, but can we guide the selection of activities so as to safeguard a family mealtime?

Though dinner may seem like the norm for a family meal, perhaps a different meal would be a better fit for the whole family. When a parent works shifts, it may be more helpful to make breakfast or lunch the family meal of the day. It is worth the effort to make a daily family meal a priority.

A family prayer before meals is important, whether we are eating in private or in public. We are thankful to God for his provision. The prayer we learned from our Catholic friends is a prayer we find Catholics know wherever they live, even outside the United States: "Bless us, O Lord, and these thy gifts, which we are about to receive from thy bounty through Christ our Lord. Amen." It is so unifying to break into that prayer with people we have just met and have all of us know it. When a young woman living with us chimed in with, "God bless the cook," we all agreed that that should be added to our prayer. It instills gratitude in the children for the efforts Mom has made to make the meal, and they really appreciate it when they are the cooks.

Family meals give us an opportunity to gather for thanksgiving, to remember what God has done for us and to share it with each other. Even young children can contribute to the conversation. This is time for us to reconnect—time for union and communion—if we deny ourselves by taking the time to make a good meal, persevering through the interruptions.

We can minimize interruptions by turning off cell phones, turning on the phone answering machine and turning off the television. We want to make the most of our time together. Meaningful conversation can be enjoyed no matter how simple the meal. Remember: "Better is a dry morsel with quiet / than a house full of feasting with strife" (Proverbs 17:1; see also Proverbs 15:17).

Healing can happen at the dinner table, for "the light of the eyes rejoices the heart, / and good news refreshes the bones" (Proverbs 15:30). Lots of laughter without negative humor (put-downs or sarcasm) helps digestion. We share "good things"—something good that happened since dinner the night before. It helps us maintain a positive focus, know more about each person's day and listen carefully to every family member. "Pleasant words are like a honeycomb, / sweetness to the soul and health to the body" (Proverbs 16:24).

Edith Schaeffer says that "relaxation, communication and a measure of beauty and pleasure should be part of even the shortest of meal breaks."[3] Even snacks can be pleasurable, especially as a way for Mom to listen to her children after a long school day. And long car rides can include nutritious snacks for a more pleasant journey for everyone, because nobody is dealing with sugar highs or lows.

Finally, we may never know fully the consequences of extending hospitality by including people at our dinner table. The writer of Hebrews urges, "Do not neglect to show hospitality to strangers, for thereby some have entertained angels unawares" (Hebrews 13:2).

AN ATTITUDE OF GRACIOUSNESS

Saint Mark gives us a glimpse into the gracious hospitality of Saint Peter's mother-in-law: "Now Simon's mother-in-law lay sick with a fever, and immediately they told him of her. And he came and took her by the hand and lifted her up, and the fever left her; and she served them" (Mark 1:30–31). As soon as this woman was well, she immediately served Jesus and Peter.

Saint Luke presents another woman who demonstrates generous hospitality toward Jesus. In Luke 10:38–42 Martha is ready to be hospitable. She graciously receives the Lord, diligent to meet the needs she perceives. Yet she struggles with growing irritation toward her sister, who is not helping her.

Her sister, Mary, on the other hand, soaks in Jesus' teaching, sitting at his feet, seemingly oblivious to Martha's preparations for the meal. Mary is distracted from the work by Jesus; Martha is "distracted" from Jesus by her work. Martha is caught up in tasks rather than in the One for whom she is performing the tasks.

Martha indulges in self-pity. She becomes self-focused, though her service is supposed to be other-focused. She subtly shifts from her serving to dissatisfaction with Mary's lack of service. She rebukes Jesus by saying, "Don't you care…?" It is her house; she wants her guests to be served well. Then she goes further—she orders Jesus to rebuke her sister.

Jesus demonstrates how much he cares by saying Martha's name twice, for emphasis. He clarifies that what she is doing is good, but that what Mary is doing is even better. In essence, Jesus rebukes Martha: "Do *you* not care about what's most important? You are caught up in details but missing the most important element—my presence! I will not disturb Mary from sitting at my feet."

Much later we have a kind of "Take Two" of this scene (see John 12:1–3). Martha again serves a banquet at her home. She is courageous, for this is a time when people want to kill her brother, Lazarus, and Jesus, yet she invites them to come for supper with other disciples.

Mary again sits at Jesus' feet. However, Martha is not anxious when Mary anoints Jesus' feet rather than helping her serve. Her gift is service, especially coupled with food. She is eager to serve Jesus without anxiety. She excels as a homemaker, and the Church now recognizes her as Saint Martha, patron saint of bakers and homemakers.

CHAPTER FIVE

Feeding the Hunger of the Heart

Have you ever noticed how the language of love seems to be the language of food? We call our special someone by names we have heard our parents use: "Honey," "Sweetie Pie," "Sugar," "Puddin' Pie!" I have heard more than one parent say to a young child, "I love you so much I could eat you up."

My youngest was a chunky six-month-old. In just one afternoon several older Italians said to me, "What a juicy baby!" "What a meaty baby!" and, "Don't you just want to bite him?!"

When David was three, he curled up on my lap and, smiling, said, "Mommy, you are yummy! You are delicious!" This is strange language, the language of food and love. This chapter will deal with the hunger of our hearts, and the next chapter will cover the food for our souls, the Eucharist.

WHY DO WE EAT?

We eat for communion, a sense of sharing with others. We eat to celebrate special days: birthdays, holidays, holy days, weddings and anniversaries. We eat because we want to enjoy the smells and flavors of delicious food. We eat to savor our connection with the past through ethnic foods shared with family and friends.

But why would we eat things they used to offer on the television show *Fear Factor?* Though the prize was enough to induce some people to eat pig uteri and bugs and worms, there is only one reason most of us eat that stuff: to sustain our lives. Bottom line: We eat for survival.

Sometimes we substitute food for love and overeat. Sometimes we misuse food in self-destructive ways to regain a sense of control we feel we have lost. What will satisfy our hunger?

In the past few decades, many people have become enmeshed in eating disorders.[1] Some react to emotional challenges by gorging themselves through overeating and then punishing themselves by making themselves vomit (bulimia).[2] Others withhold food from themselves (anorexia) as if they are not worth the food they would consume to maintain their lives.[3] Those who struggle with these disorders often suffer heroically. The Lord says to each of us, "*I love you! I made you, and I want you to eat the food I provide for you. You are worth feeding!*"

Sometimes we try to control others by feeding them when they are not hungry. We ply them with false guilt about our hard work fixing the food or about children who may be starving in another country. We challenge them to be members of the Clean Plate Club when we may have served them too much food. Instead we should teach them how to take smaller portions and then ask for seconds. We need to balance not throwing away good food and not forcing children to overeat.

Many Americans face weight challenges. On my way to a Weight Watchers meeting, I asked God to help me battle my body. Mid-sentence I realized that that was not a helpful prayer—it was producing conflict. We do not want our minds to battle our bodies but rather to befriend them. Our goal is to unite our heads (what we know to be true) with our bodies (how we want to live that truth).

We want to love ourselves with greater self-control, finding joy in the sacrifices we make to lose weight for the greater goal of good health. Since we only have taste buds in our mouths, we need to slow down our eating and savor the flavor! We want the peace of knowing we are doing what we can so that we can serve the Lord and our families for as long as we can.

Personally, I want to recommend highly Weight Watchers for the practical program for life they promote.[4] The meetings are encouraging, with helpful strategies for handling difficult situations. They offer words of encouragement as we try to identify and to change family eating patterns before our children struggle with weight issues. They provide recipe ideas so that we can cook for the family and help ourselves at the same time. And the leaders work with pregnant and nursing women in a very positive way, so they can regain their shape while nurturing their children.

FOOD IS A GIFT
Food is a gift from God, but like any gift, we must use it well. Overeating, the sin of gluttony, is one of the seven deadly sins (see *CCC*, 1866). The definition of eating more than we need will differ from person to person. We need to ask Jesus to be Lord of our appetites. The fruit of the Spirit of self-control helps us be moderate with food.

Mortification is an important aspect of connecting self-control with regard to food and your prayer life. Saint Josemaría Escrivá said, "Unless you mortify yourself you'll never be a prayerful soul."[5] However, he added this caution, "Choose mortifications that don't mortify others."[6] Even mortification requires moderation. His suggestions include simple things like forgoing salt on food, sugar in tea or a second helping and choosing the smaller piece of meat, without calling attention to the sacrifice.

Warning: All foods are "clean," but some Christians are too weak to see you eat or drink certain things without falling into sin.

> Let us then pursue what makes for peace and for mutual upbuilding. Do not, for the sake of food, destroy the work of God. Everything is indeed clean, but it is wrong for any one to make others fall by what he eats; it is right not to eat meat or drink wine or do anything that makes your brother stumble. (Romans 14:19–21)

Try to strengthen everyone. For example, if you are with a friend who is an alcoholic, choose not to drink alcohol in front of him or her. Love for others is much more important than your "right" to a particular food or drink. As Saint Paul says, "So, whether you eat or drink, or whatever you do, do all to the glory of God" (1 Corinthians 10:31).

CHAPTER SIX

A Mother's Guide to the Eucharist

God provides food that is needful. In the Old Testament there are three examples of God's provision of food for his people that reveal important truths about the spiritual food he gives us in the Eucharist: the Passover, the daily provision of manna for God's people in the desert and the *Todah* sacrifice in the temple.

PASSOVER

In order for the angel of death to "pass over" their homes, Moses describes what the Israelites have to do. They are to kill an unblemished lamb, spread its blood over the lintel and then cook and eat the whole lamb (see Exodus 12:5–13). Only those Israelites who observe the Lord's Passover will preserve their firstborn son's life.

Jesus is the Lamb of God who takes away the sin of the world, Saint John announces at Christ's Baptism. Like the Passover sacrifice, Jesus has died, he covers us with his blood, and he calls us to feast on him at each eucharistic celebration. "For Christ, our Paschal [Passover] Lamb, has been sacrificed. Let us, therefore, celebrate the festival" (1 Corinthians 5:7–8).

MANNA

After the Exodus the Israelites wander in the wilderness for forty years. God provides miraculous daily bread (see Exodus 16:14–15), which the people call "manna."

Jesus contrasts the manna the Israelites received with the gift of life he offers:

> I am the bread of life. Your fathers ate the manna in the wilderness, and they died. This is the bread which comes down from heaven, that a man may eat of it and not die. I am the living bread which came down from heaven; if any one eats of this bread, he will live for ever; and the bread which I shall give for the life of the world is my flesh. (John 6:48–51)

Jesus is the living bread of God.

THE *TODAH* SACRIFICE

The *Todah* was the only sacrifice in the old covenant that would never end. It was literally a sacrifice of "thanksgiving." An example of this is found in Psalm 50:14–15:

> Offer to God a sacrifice of thanksgiving,
> and pay your vows to the Most High;
> and call upon me in the day of trouble;
> I will deliver you, and you shall glorify me.

This passage reveals the following pattern: Someone recounts his peril; he cries out to the Lord; he promises to offer the *Todah* when God answers.

When the Lord delivers the person, the petitioner takes to the temple a lamb for sacrifice and bread to be consecrated. This is the only consecrated bread that laypeople can eat. Then he gathers his family and friends to share the consecrated bread and a cup of wine, declaring the Lord's salvation so that all can share in the thanksgiving.

Does that sound familiar? Jesus "gave thanks" (from the Greek word *eucharisteo*), blessed bread, broke it and shared it with his disciples, saying, "'This is my body which is given for you. Do this in remembrance of me.'" And likewise the chalice after supper, saying, "'This chalice which is poured out for you is the new covenant in my blood'" (Luke 22:19–20).

The sacrifice of the Mass is our covenant meal, renewing our covenant with God in thanksgiving for all he has done for us. "The Holy Spirit who thus awakens the memory of the Church then inspires thanksgiving and praise (*doxology*)" (*CCC*, 1103). Once the Spirit awakens our spirits, we respond with songs and prayers, staying to offer a "thanksgiving" after Mass, rather than making a fifty-yard dash to the parking lot!

We offer ourselves at Mass through the gift of bread and wine. Through the words of consecration spoken by the priest *in persona Christi*, the Holy Spirit transforms the bread and wine into the very Body and Blood of our crucified, resurrected and ascended Lord. Jesus, our high priest in heaven, perpetually offers himself, the once-for-all sacrifice on our altar for us to adore and to receive.

In imitation of Christ, we are called to be living sacrifices. We leave Mass to continue our mission to love and to serve the Lord. Through our ordinary work done in his extraordinary grace, we return home to love and to serve our families.

May we share Jesus at the table of the Lord and then be strengthened to serve our families at our table at home. And may our dinnertimes reflect our thanksgiving for the grace our Lord has lavished on us.

PART THREE

*She
rises
while
it is still
night*

CHAPTER SEVEN

Rhythm of Life:
The Dance of Time Management

Time management is like a dance. We try to maintain our balance while we adjust to the ever-changing rhythm of life. Before we examine our use of time, we want to recognize the gift of time.

Time is a gift—these minutes will never occur again. They cannot be stored like money in the bank or clothes in our closet. There may be millions of moments left in our lives, but we cannot presume to know how many are left. We do not have to be quantifiably productive every minute, but we want to live these minutes well.

We look at the present moment in the light of eternity, for the Lord "has put eternity into man's mind" (Ecclesiastes 3:11). We were made to live forever, so right now counts. Eternity puts time into context. Saint Paul wrote, "I have been crucified with Christ; it is no longer I who live, but Christ who lives in me; and the life I now live in the flesh I live by faith in the Son of God, who loved me and gave himself for me" (Galatians 2:20).

With an eternal perspective, we realize we are not living for ourselves but living for Christ.

So, *when* do we do God's will, living for Christ? We can only do it in the present moment. *Now* is the moment that eternity touches our lives. *Now* is the moment of grace, of repentance, of choosing to live to please God. Each moment is its own unique opportunity for a fresh start, a new beginning.

The Proverbs 31 woman demonstrates wisdom in managing time. "She rises while it is yet night / and provides food for her household / and tasks for her maidens" (Proverbs 31:15). The wisdom we need to make decisions is greatly enhanced through the gifts of the Holy Spirit, which we receive through the sacrament of Confirmation.

DISCIPLINED TO RISE EARLY

Why does this woman rise early in the morning, while it is still dark? She begins her day with prayer. Like the psalmist, she says, "But I, O LORD, cry to you; / in the morning my prayer comes before you" (Psalm 88:13); or, "I rise before dawn and cry for help; / I hope in your words" (Psalm 119:147).

So many psalms speak of rising early to greet the Lord. Morning persons have probably underlined those verses. The rest of us who are night owls may have assumed these verses applied only to naturally early risers! However, we all need to spend time with the Lord in prayer at the beginning of the day—early birds and night owls alike.

In spiritual direction Father Ray Ryland, a dear friend and spiritual mentor, illustrated the importance of prayer in the morning. He compared sleep to a little death in which we lose consciousness as we relinquish our control, and rising the next day to a little resurrection. Our prayer time reminds us of who God is, who we are and why we are doing what we are doing.

Let me hear in the morning of your merciful love,
for in you I put my trust.

Teach me the way I should go,
for to you I lift up my soul. (Psalm 143:8)

Prayer in the morning is part of our preparation for meeting our household's needs; we need to get our bearings before we are bombarded. Time for prayer is like scuba diving in the midst of a storm; it is peaceful below the storm, if we go deep enough: "O Lord, in the morning you hear my voice; / in the morning I prepare a sacrifice for you, and watch" (Psalm 5:3).

When things are very difficult, we recall all that the Lord has already done for us and that he does not change even though our circumstances do.

But this I call to mind,
and therefore I have hope:

The steadfast love of the Lord never ceases,
his mercies never come to an end;
they are new every morning;
great is your faithfulness.
"The Lord is my portion," says my soul,
"therefore I will hope in him." (Lamentations 3:21–24)

This is not wishful thinking. This is a sure hope, a greater reality than what we can see. We need to grasp—and be grasped by—this truth first thing in the morning, to establish our day. Our confidence is in the Lord; every morning he renews his promises to us.

Family prayers are helpful too. As the psalmist says, "Satisfy us in the morning with your mercy, / that we may rejoice and be glad all our days" (Psalm 90:14). Yes, morning prayer applies to the family as well, yet family prayer cannot substitute for time alone with the Lord.

WHEN WILL WE PRAY?

We are more likely to pray if we set a specific time for prayer. Unlike the sluggard who turns on his bed like a door on hinges (see Proverbs 26:14), we set our alarm and rise. Saint Josemaría Escrivá refers to this as the heroic moment: "Conquer yourself each day from the very first moment, getting up on the dot, at a set time, without granting a single minute to laziness. If, with the help of God, you conquer yourself in that moment, you'll have accomplished a great deal for the rest of the day."[1]

Barring unusual circumstances, such as a wakeful baby, a sick child or an illness, we should rise at a set time. In the midst of an early morning stupor, it is best not to question the decision made the night before. No negotiations! There are seasons of life when we cannot live by the alarm clock; however, many of us can determine an appropriate rising time.

Regarding when to pray, the *Catechism* urges us, "One does not undertake contemplative prayer only when one has the time: one makes time for the Lord, with the firm determination not to give up, no matter what trials and dryness one may encounter" (*CCC*, 2710). We do not pray because it is convenient or because we feel like it. We pray because we can approach our loving heavenly Father as his beloved child.

WHERE WILL WE PRAY?

A college friend responded to my query as to her morning prayer time, "I was prostrate at the bedside chapel," meaning, "I was asleep." It is hard to stay focused when lying in bed!

Jesus chose a change of location to limit interruptions. After healing and teaching late into the night, he still rose early to pray alone. "And when it was day he departed and went into a lonely place" (Luke 4:42). He was busy, yet he took time to pray—and he was perfect! How much more do we need time for recollected prayer?

Jesus demonstrates the power of prayer in his life, teaching the disciples:

> But when you pray, go into your room and shut the door and pray to your Father who is in secret; and your Father who sees in secret will reward you.
>
> And in praying do not heap up empty phrases as the Gentiles do; for they think that they will be heard for their many words. Do not be like them, for your Father knows what you need before you ask him. (Matthew 6:6–8)

Jesus teaches the necessity of private space for prayer as well as the importance of thoughtful mental prayer that is specific about our needs.

A place for prayer matters—away from the phone and a bed. Once I designated a place, I became consistent with morning prayer. I organized materials to assist me in prayer in an attractive bag that matches the colors of the living room, where it remains next to a comfortable chair. I can easily shift it when necessary.

The materials I like to use include my Bible, a copy of *Magnificat*[2] or *The Word Among Us*,[3] index cards for memorizing Scripture verses (reference on one side, text on the other, for easy review), a *Catechism*, a prayer journal for recording requests and thanksgivings, a pen, a rosary and a biography of a saint or other spiritual reading. No more wasting time hunting for these items. When I travel I take the whole bag, so that all of the materials are available. I take it to a weekly Holy Hour or sometimes toss it in the car when I expect to have free time during a child's sports practice.

FOR WHAT DO WE PRAY?

We ask for God's blessing on our work: "Commit your work to the LORD, / and your plans will be established" (Proverbs 16:3). We acknowledge him as the Lord of time. We give him our plans, hopes and dreams for the day and ask him to lead us to do those things that he desires. We actively yield our will to his.

Placing our trust in the Lord at the outset of the day helps us to set the plans for the day and yet allow for flexibility. We can start the day on Plan A and feel as if we are on Plan E by breakfast! I remind myself daily, *There is all the time I need today to do God's will today.* Prayer is an essential part of that reminder. We are not coming to God and telling him our agenda; rather we are coming to share our hearts and to hear his.

In the midst of prayer, what do we do with distracting thoughts? We can jot down the miscellaneous "to dos" that crowd our thinking. Rather than leaving our prayer to do a task, unless it is urgent, or ignoring a thought about something we really do need to remember, we can use a Post-it—getting it on paper and off our mind. This frees us to return to prayer with focused attention.

In his book *Appointment With God,* Father Michael Scanlan mentions including at least five minutes of silence to listen to God, noting any inspirations that come as additional tasks for the day (for example, speak to this person, write this thank-you note, offer a meal to this family). Then we ask the Lord to show us where in our schedule we could include these tasks, if they are his will. Time for silence and inspirations is part of the work of the Holy Spirit in our lives.

Prayer in the morning is the beginning of a day of prayer. As Saint Paul stresses, "Pray at all times in the Spirit" (Ephesians 6:18). When we consecrate the day, our various tasks become prayer as well. Priority loving leads to priority living.

INTERRUPTIONS

We do not pray *instead of* caring for our family; we pray *as a vital way to* care for our family. We receive God's grace in order to be a channel of that grace to them. We receive God's love in order to express that love to them. We receive God's word instructing us how to act toward our loved ones throughout the day. We remember who we are in Christ so we can lovingly remind them who they are in Christ.

Your family benefits from a time of prayer, though you may need a plan for dealing with interruptions, since some children have a kind of radar once mom is stirring. Can you give your children a time before which they are not allowed to get out of bed? If they cannot read the clock yet, can you train them to wait until someone comes for them? Perhaps your husband can be "on call" for early risers, so that you are guaranteed time to pray for even fifteen minutes.

In some seasons of life, your prayer time may coincide with an early-morning nursing, after which both you and your baby return to bed. Rising early can be difficult, especially if you have wakened throughout the night. You have a soul that will live forever in a body with limitations. In various seasons of life, you will have certain physical restrictions. However, the earlier your prayer time, the better for everyone; the further you get into the day, the harder it is to regroup and make time for prayer.

Sometimes an interruption in prayer will have more to do with our emotional state, a struggle we are having in approaching God. We need to discern prayer time as an invitation from our Lord, in imitation of his prayer, to have childlike trust in our heavenly Father. In Jesus' moment of greatest agony in the Garden of Gethsemane, he poured out his heart: "Father, if you are willing, remove this chalice from me; nevertheless not my will, but yours, be done" (Luke 22:42). In these moments of greatest challenge, we remember that we can approach the throne of our heavenly Father and find mercy, regardless of our feelings.

A helpful word picture is a train: The engine represents the facts about God, who I am in Christ and what is this vocation to which I am called; the cargo car represents my faith connected to the facts (the engine can run with or without my faith); and the caboose represents my feelings—nice but unnecessary. Our feelings of sadness, unresolved relational difficulties, frustration and depression can derail the train. We get back on track by beginning with good theology and placing our faith where it belongs.

An example of someone who did just that is Mother Teresa of Calcutta. A recently published book of her letters reveals that she experienced about fifty years of a dark night of the soul without the consolations of faith. Through all of that time, she persisted in placing her faith in what she knew to be true rather than in her feelings of emptiness.[4]

TIME FOR OTHER SPIRITUAL COMMITMENTS

Besides prayer, you want to receive the grace of the sacraments. How frequently do you want to schedule Confession?

Mass? Through your diocese's Web site you can discover your options for both sacraments at local parishes. Perhaps your spouse can help you (and vice versa) to take advantage of what is available. You can also share this information with others.

When you are unable to go to Mass, make an act of spiritual communion: "I wish, my Lord, to receive you with the purity, humility and devotion with which your most holy mother received you, in the spirit and fervor of the saints."[5]

Can you include time to learn more about the Faith on your own, through an adult education class or through a Bible study at your parish? The prophet Hosea warns,

> My people are destroyed for lack of knowledge;
>> because you have rejected knowledge,
>> I reject you from being a priest to me.
> And since you have forgotten the law of your God,
>> I also will forget your children. (Hosea 4:6)

Growing in knowledge of the Faith is essential. Unless you know God and his law, you cannot be faithful. You will be destroyed for lack of knowledge, and your children will be affected by it; however, if you feed your mind with truth, you will bless your family.

Recognizing the need for Catholic Scripture studies, Scott and I founded the St. Paul Center for Biblical Theology in 2001. We have developed downloadable online Bible studies, and we offer training for laypeople to be able to present studies entitled "Genesis to Jesus," "The Bible and the Mass," "The Bible and the Blessed Virgin Mary" and "The Bible and the Sacraments."[6]

Growing numbers of Catholic Bible studies are available for laypeople. Jeff Cavins has produced *The Great Adventure*,[7] an overview of salvation history. Emmaus Road Publishing has Bible studies available for small group study,[8] as does Catholic Scriptire Studies,[9] and Ignatius Press is publishing a study Bible with individual fascicles that are outstanding for individual or small group study.[10]

Is there a pastor near you who offers spiritual direction? Spiritual direction, coupled with Confession, can be a powerful tool to help you understand your patterns of sin so that you can take incremental steps to change your heart and mind. It also increases accountability on your path to holiness.

Is there a retreat available? Could you help another woman attend by offering a ride or perhaps a scholarship? Retreats are rare opportunities to disconnect from ordinary life and to regroup spiritually—many women have not yet discovered how rejuvenating retreats can be.

Prayer is essential for setting the tone of the day. Yet your home is not a monastery; you have an active household. Your life of prayer is lived in conformity with your vocation. You cannot excuse neglecting your loved ones for a prayer commitment any more than you can justify neglecting prayer to care for your family's needs.

WHEN DO YOU MEET YOUR OTHER NEEDS?
Once the structure for your spiritual life is on the schedule, examine your physical needs for rest and food in your rhythm of life.

When should your day begin? That is your rising time. How much sleep do you need? Work backward from when your day needs to begin, and you have your bedtime. The need for sleep varies for each person; it does not matter if you know someone who only needs six hours, if you really need eight. Be honest with yourself.

What about meals? You need to ensure proper nutrition, especially when you are pregnant or nursing. How much time should you factor for meal preparation, consumption and cleanup? Just because no one else is home for lunch does not mean you should skip that meal. And if you are more of a grazer than a three-meal-a-day volume eater, how much time do you need to plan these smaller but nutritious meals?

What regimen of exercise will help you be healthy? Can you walk a track, the neighborhood or the mall with your spouse or a good friend? (When I talk while I walk, I do not even feel as if I have been exercising, plus I have had time with someone special.) You may want to borrow an exercise video from the library and make it a fun time with your children while they romp around the family room, laughing at the funny faces you are making and odd movements you are attempting. After all, "health and soundness are better than all gold, / and a robust body than countless riches. / There is no wealth better than health of body, / and there is no gladness above joy of heart" (Sirach 30:15–16).

TIME WITH YOUR SPOUSE

The next priority to schedule is time with your spouse, developing your relationship. Time together could include an early morning walk for prayer and conversation, provided you have children old enough to leave at home alone for twenty to thirty minutes. Perhaps you could sit on the couch when your spouse first gets home from work or right after dinner, so the children can see you enjoying each other.

It is important to keep dating one another. Maybe there are other couples in your financial situation who would be willing to swap babysitting every other weekend so you are guaranteed two date nights a month without paying a sitter. For several years my parents gave us date money to encourage us to date without having to budget for it.

Your spouse may not initiate asking you out for a date. In dating I do not think that girls should pursue guys; but once married, there is nothing wrong with a wife's initiating a date. For a time in our early marriage, I pouted that Scott did not ask me out much, until I realized that I had a choice: I could be upset and not go out, or I could talk with him about it, make the arrangements with the sitter and enjoy the time together. After all, I was thinking about a sitter and knew who was available. It was a pride thing—I still wanted to be courted; however, I needed to believe that Scott wanted to be with me and was happy to spend the time and money for us to be together. Since his mind was full of other things, while dating was on my heart, it only made sense to bring it up to him. I am glad I did!

We also need time for reunion, a plan for intimacy. Regardless of commercials to the contrary, spontaneity is not all it is cracked up to be. Look for ways to love each other, including making time for the act of marriage.

Time for Your Children

The next priority is time spent developing a relationship with each child. One of the challenges Scott and I face is parenting children of a variety of ages at the same time. At one point we had older children who liked to talk late at night, a baby up throughout the night and young children rising at dawn. We wondered if we were young enough to do this!

Home is the place for us to communicate unconditional love to each child, especially through conversation "of the sort that takes place around fireplaces, washing dishes together, having tea together, eating together, walking together, and discovering things in common together."[11] Whether we dip cookies in milk and discuss life with a young one, share a treat with a teen after school or make a lunch and shopping date with an older child, we have opportunities to glimpse our child's world. Sometimes it is easier to work alongside each other in the garden and talk, or sit side by side with a teen in a car, than to talk face-to-face across a table (unless you are teaching him or her to drive, and you are raising your voice as you use your imaginary brakes!).

We want to do more than take care of our children. We want to get to know them by spending time together and enjoying them. We look for a balance of work and play.

Different families do different things well. What is natural for your family? For our family, work together is more natural for us than play. When our oldest ones were little, I had to include on my list of tasks for the day, get on the floor and play Duplos (Lego blocks) with the boys. I wanted to play with them, but I was more inclined to get work done.

You might always choose to play, so you have to get more work done. You may know of a family that seems more spiritual than yours or one that does more music or more athletics than yours. Rather than judge your family against others, discern your strengths and thank the Lord for them. Then learn what you can from others and add what is needed for a more balanced family life.

Care for our relationships with our children includes praying for them and with them. We have family prayer in the morning, and we pray the rosary after dinner. We want realistic expectations depending on the ages of our children. For example, when our family was young, we prayed an after-dinner decade of the rosary every night, which took three and a half minutes, instead of a full rosary, which entailed a twenty-minute ordeal of keeping little ones peaceful and therefore rarely happened. When our children grew older, we adjusted to a full rosary after dinner. We set a smaller goal that we could accomplish and then built from there.

Be careful not to substitute religious activities for enjoying your children, or they could react negatively when they are older. Instead of starting with a Holy Hour with a child, could you make a five-minute visit after Mass and build to a fifteen-minute visit midweek? These are disciplines that can grow over long periods of time.

Sometimes when my dad wanted to gather the family to pray, my mom would wisely ask, "When was the last time you played with them?" If it had been a while, he would ask who wanted to play kickball and then head outside with us instead of insisting on a prayer time. Mom's theory was, if you play as much as you pray, children will not resent times of prayer; Dad concurred, and we were grateful he did.

Spending time with children includes being with them first thing in the morning, at meals throughout the day and at bedtime. When we rise first, we are ready to greet them; we are ahead of the action with and for the family. We establish a rhythm for the day through our meals together and regular bedtime routines.

We express love to our children in ways that are natural to us and to them. Dr. Gary Chapman explains five ways love is expressed in his book *The Five Love Languages:*

1. *Quality time:* talk in person or by phone; say, "I love you."
2. *Physical touch and closeness:* a pat on the back, a hug, a good-night kiss, a night blessing with hands on head, a back rub, a tickle, a walk while holding hands.
3. *Act of service*: besides the acts of service I already intend to do for someone, I include something he or she specifically mentions for me to do.
4. *A word of affirmation*: at least one genuine compliment each day.
5. *Gift-giving*: some little gift or note each week (for example, for children living independently— coupons, leftovers, an extra box of tissues in winter or lip balm, an E-mail expressing thanks for something done for the family).[12]

To help me track whether or not I am expressing all five love languages to each child and my spouse at least once a week, I have made an insert for my planner. Though a checklist may seem contrived, especially if we have not been this intentional about how we express love before now, it helps us stay on track for doing what we intend to do. We want to express love in every possible way so that our spouse and each child know how really and truly they are loved. We want them to *feel* loved. It is as if we are making deposits in an emotional bank account, which is very necessary before we make withdrawals.

With very young children, we may not be able to discern what their primary love language might be, so it is most helpful to speak all five languages to them. While we tune in to the love language that is natural to each person, the goal is to be "multilingual."

TIME FOR YOUR TASKS AS A PROVIDER— ORDINARY TIME

Ordinary time—what does that mean? It is the normal, everyday type of religious day (for all days are religious, though not all days are meant for fasting or feasting). Ordinary time marks the day-in, day-out challenge of living for the Lord, being faithful to the mundane tasks. In ordinary time we plod along, doing the next thing that needs to be done, knowing that even that nondescript day is part of our long obedience in the same direction.

Though Scott and I are continually grateful for each other, typically we do not rise in the morning with ecstatic honeymoon-type utterances of "I love you with all of my heart!" or "I can't believe I'm married to you!" Rather we rise to the tasks of the day, demonstrating our love and faithfulness as we do ordinary things that need to be done.

Likewise, the birth of a child brings great joy and wonderment. Yet life is not lived in the thrill of the birth, no matter how much we love this child. We do not usually greet our children at breakfast saying, "I am your mother!" or, "You're my beloved daughter!" or, "I'm so grateful for a son like you!" It would be great if we verbalized our feelings more often, but ordinary life, in general, is not lived that way.

There is a reason why there is more "ordinary" time in a liturgical year than special days. More of life is lived in the ordinary, while the extraordinary enlarges our understanding of the ordinary. In the next chapter we will look at ways we can schedule time for the tasks that make up the majority of our ordinary days in family life.

CHAPTER EIGHT

Waltzing Through Life:
Establishing a Pattern to Our Tasks

When the Proverbs 31 woman rises early in the morning, she places the care of her household over her own comfort. She does what each of us hopes to do: Provide an overall structure to daily tasks so that our families do not just *survive* but rather *thrive.* Our goal, in service to Christ, is to meet the physical, psychological, emotional and spiritual needs of each family member. We want to create a home that is a haven of rest, a safe harbor from the storms of life in which we welcome family members.

A planner is a useful tool for organizing time for tasks. It is an indispensable tool for efficient household management, since time is so valuable. Your planner needs to be user-friendly, taking a minimum amount of time to maintain. To best fit your needs and lifestyle, you can choose either an electronic or a paper version. If you use it well, a planner can save time, limit stacks of paper, keep information handy and provide you with a daily focus.

A planner limits stacks of paper. My goal is to touch paper coming into my home no more than twice. First, I read the material and highlight important information. Next, I record minimal details of an event in my planner. Last, I file the paper, form, sheet of directions, invitation, newsletter or related article in a standing file near my phone, one file for each activity (class, sport, club) for me and for each of the children. Filed in alphabetical order, it is easy to grab and check details too numerous to copy into the planner (such as directions to a destination), yet it keeps the information at my fingertips.

A planner keeps information handy. Instead of searching through scattered notes and thoughts, I spend my time doing what needs to be done. I designate pages of my planner for Christmas and birthday gift ideas when loved ones make suggestions. I list ideas for future liturgical celebrations on one page and vacation ideas and places on another. I jot ideas for future study topics or recommended spiritual reading for easy reference. I also list clothing and shoe sizes of family members (updated regularly) to assist efficient shopping.

A planner maintains focus for the day. If I list projects and designate specific times to accomplish that day's tasks beforehand, I have a focus for that day. The planner helps me to direct my attention and energy toward those tasks in a given time frame. I can always adjust, but utilizing the planner keeps me moving forward.

One of my challenges is estimating how much time a task will take, including time to set up, clean up or travel. I tend to try to squeeze everything I can out of each minute. The result? I'm often late. In the interest of maximizing my time, I overbook the space, misjudge the time and make someone else wait. This is a major flaw I am working on, because I do not want to communicate what, in fact, some people feel—that their time is not valuable to me. I have to accept the limitations of time and adjust to it. If I double my first estimate of how much time something will take, I am more accurate. I am also trying to change my thinking from "I will do one more task before I leave" to "I will take a task with me so I leave on time." If I have extra time wherever I am going, I have a task with me, so time is not wasted.

The other consequence of poor time estimation is how often I require an adrenaline rush in order to move from one commitment to the next: racing through the house, grabbing the keys, jumping into the car and hoping I do not back into the brick wall as I floor it out of the driveway. (My children tease that Cruella De Vil drives like me!) I create unnecessary stress for my children as well as for myself. I may save seconds, but they are hardly worth the anxiety of rushing, the frustration of traffic and then the disappointment of being late (again!). I need to put others first in my time management, which will contribute to peace in our home. I take this thought to heart, "Do your work before the appointed time, / and in God's time he will give you your reward" (Sirach 51:30).

ESTABLISH A WEEKLY PATTERN

Group tasks together so that certain days are designated for laundry, errands, cleaning or bills. Then family members will know when to ask you to run an errand or which day they can anticipate having clean clothes. If you do all financial tasks at one time—paying bills for the week, stamping the bills for the next day's mail, filing the receipts for tax purposes and balancing the checkbook—you can streamline the process, finishing the task and freeing yourself from thinking about financial things for the rest of the week.

The planner can help you schedule all of your regular activities as well as those of your spouse and children. You can create a master schedule of school and extracurricular activities, including sports practices and games, music lessons and performances, altar serving, scouting and other clubs and hobbies. This helps you track related details of life, such as when you are providing the carpool, when you need cleaned uniforms, when forms are due for the next outing or sports' season or when certain materials are required to finish a project (such as a cake mix for the Great Cake Bake-off for Cub Scouts).

Once regularly scheduled activities are noted, identify blocks of unscheduled time. (Yes, they do exist!) These open time periods can be designated for other tasks of the day. (More details about homemaking tasks are included in chapters ten and eleven.)

REMEMBER THE LORD'S DAY

The Lord's Day sets the tone for the week. The Jews were expected to work for six days and then worship and rest on the seventh; Christians worship and rest every seventh day— on the first day of the week—and then work six days. We are sabbatarian creatures; we cannot work all seven days a week and still be healthy people.

To honor the Sabbath and keep it holy is one of the Ten Commandments (see Exodus 20:8–11; Deuteronomy 5:12–15). It is rooted in the covenant of creation and in remembrance of the liberation of the Israelites from bondage. It is transformed into the Lord's Day by Jesus' Resurrection on the first day of the week of the new creation and in remembrance of the liberation of his people from the bondage of sin (see *CCC*, 2174). We are not to treat the Lord's Day as a day of work for ourselves or for others. The Lord's Day is a time of respite from work and of renewal through worship.

This is an essential part of the rhythm of life. We celebrate these sacred mysteries, uniting heaven and earth in worship and praise, in the sacrifice of the Mass. This is why it is such a serious sin to miss Mass intentionally on a Sunday (see *CCC*, 2181). The writer of Hebrews warns us not to neglect our salvation: "For if the message declared by angels was valid and every transgression or disobedience received a just retribution, how shall we escape if we neglect such a great salvation?" (Hebrews 2:2–3).

Even more, we worship on the Lord's Day not as a duty to be performed but as a "*response* to the Lord's loving initiative" (*CCC*, 2062). We prioritize Sunday Mass with our families. At Mass our faith is strengthened, and we remember God's saving work in our lives. Our hope is renewed, and we trust that the Lord is at work in our lives even in the midst of suffering. And our love for the Lord is deepened, hearing his Word read and receiving his Word in the Eucharist.

Not only do you give this day to the Lord, but he gives it back to you as a day of relaxation with family and friends. (For students, your studies are your work; set aside studying for that day, though be sure to do studies the rest of the week.) It is a guilt-free, work-free day for hospitality, letter writing, playing an instrument, taking a walk, napping or whatever refreshes you.

The Day of Preparation

Just as Friday is the day of preparation for the Jews' Sabbath, Saturday is our day of preparation for the Lord's Day. We think about and prepare for our Sunday meal, so that we do not have to purchase groceries on Sunday and make store employees work. We lay out good clothes so that we are sure they are clean and ironed ahead of time. We write our tithe check. And many of us go to Confession so that we are ready to receive our Lord in the Eucharist.

Family Meetings

Some families have a family meeting at the end of the Lord's Day, in order to prepare for the week ahead. The DuBois family holds a meeting each Sunday evening to coordinate their weekly schedules. (This works well with older children, especially if they drive.) They double-check plans and note schedule changes and additional needs. They share specific tasks with which they need assistance and factor these tasks into the overall schedule. As they combine needs and desires with the realities of the week, they work together, contributing to the peace of their home.

A family meeting also helps us coordinate irregular needs: car repairs, medical and dental appointments, special liturgical celebrations, care for yards and gardens and overall maintenance of the home. With our planners in hand, we can list the concerns of family members. By designating a time to meet their needs, we communicate how important their needs are to us. This kind of proactive planning strengthens the bond of love in the family.

MANAGE THE SCHEDULE

It is one thing to make a schedule; it is another to maintain it. Our routines create the framework to unify our goals and dreams with reality, provided we follow our routines. Experts say it takes at least three weeks to establish a new habit, so it is best if we commit to our schedule for a minimum of three weeks before we tweak it.

Sometimes we feel as if we do not have enough time to make a schedule, but that is as foolish as saying we cannot make a budget because we do not have enough money. Time, like money, needs to be spent well. Holly Pierlot writes, "Schedules might be limiting,…but disorder is more limiting."[1]

Creating a schedule is like setting a boundary, a fence around the yard so that our family can work and play in a safe environment. Maintaining the schedule is like making sure the fence posts are solid and the wood slats are affixed well. There is freedom, not restriction, in organization. When we identify the priorities of our lives and set a well-managed schedule to live those priorities, we bring peace to our homes. We discover that uncluttered thinking results from uncluttered time and space. (You will find more about uncluttered space in chapters ten and eleven.)

Having a schedule allows time and space for contemplation, instead of just running from task to task. For homemakers, mortification may be doing what must be done next, regardless of our feelings. It means putting down one unfinished project we may really enjoy to do a carpool that has been scheduled.

As we assist our family members in scheduling time, part of our success is our ability to enable others to succeed—our spouse, our children and any workers who help us. Like the Proverbs 31 woman, we care for those in our charge, recruiting them as part of the team in accomplishing the work of housework so that all benefit from peace and order.

A tremendous resource for time management is *Time Management From the Inside Out* by Julie Morgenstern. She applies a similar strategy to both time and space management. She encourages us to envision the overall schedule we want and to list our long-term financial and interpersonal goals (with our spouse, if we are married). How do we make the ideal real? We get specific.

This broader planning is accomplished through incremental steps. Under each long-range dream, we write specific goals that will move us closer to fulfilling our dreams. These goals are subdivided into "S.M.A.R.T. goals": *S*pecific (concrete), *M*easurable (when and where it can happen), *A*ction-oriented (specific actions), *R*ealistic (reasonable) and *T*imely (doable). [2] Once we have a list of more easily attainable goals, we examine our limitations of money (when will our budget enable us to accomplish the goals?) and time (when will our schedule include the time needed to achieve the goals?). Then we know how to proceed, enjoying the satisfaction of realizing our dreams, little by little.

Once my overall schedule is set for the fall or spring school semester or for summer, I need to plan for the week. I set aside an hour and a half on Sunday night to review the week's schedule and specify tasks for certain days. I decide on deadlines to move various projects ahead by one or two steps. I include a fifteen-minute block of time each night to prioritize tasks for the next day, following Father Michael Scanlan's method he shared with me during spiritual direction: *A* means Act today; *B* means Best if I could do it today; *C* means Could do it this week if possible; *D* means Delegate it to someone else; and *E* means Eliminate it. If more than one item uses the same letter, Father Scanlan recommends adding numbers to further prioritize. This is the list to take to prayer the next morning. Then an insight or inspiration may either change the priorities or even add to them.

Another small idea has helped me (as an incurable list maker): I use small Post-it notes, one per call to be made, errand to be run or e-mail to send. If I do the task, I throw the note away; if not, I move it to the date I will do it, without rewriting it. I am saving time by not recopying lists to neaten them, and I am limiting (false) feelings of guilt for not completing the page of to-dos.

CHANGES IN THE SEASONS OF LIFE

In the vocation of marriage, women experience many seasons of life. You might be a bride who is still adjusting to sharing life with an adult of the opposite sex. You might be a young mother with a toddler and a nursing baby, wondering if you will ever sleep through the night again. You might be a busy mother of a half dozen children with a spread of ages that stretches you daily between toddlers and teens. You might be adjusting to an empty nest and life with an older spouse without children around. Or perhaps you are living your advanced years independently now that your spouse is gone.

Since women vary in their season of life, we do not look for a one-size-fits-all structure to a schedule. However, principles of time organization can be helpful no matter what our stage in life.

One question we all face at each stage of life is, How do I deal with a sense of failure? We might have a wonderful meal on the table and the laundry might be done, but there could be messy corners in the house. Or we might have meaningful conversations with our spouse and children but forget our family prayer time.

We face an impossible task, *if it means that everything has to be finished every night*. I do not think we can complete every task every day; God does not ask us to, because he does not ask us to do the impossible. That means that this vocation is an opportunity to embrace humility in knowing that we cannot do it all. So we gauge what is possible for that day and ask him for the strength to do it and the wisdom to adjust our goals, and then we thank him for what we are able to do. "For everything there is a season, and a time for every matter under heaven" (Ecclesiastes 3:1). Every season of life is an opportunity to serve the Lord.

Some questions on my mind recently are, How could Jesus sleep at night? How did he manage to wait thirty years before he began his three-year public ministry? And once he began his ministry, how could he go to bed knowing that every disease had not been healed, every demon had not been cast out, every truth had not been taught?

There is only way he could do it: Jesus yielded his will to his Father. He accepted the limitations of his human body, which needed food and sleep. He trusted his Father's timing, and so must we.

In different seasons of life, we adjust for temporary imbalances. Are there special circumstances? A move, a new baby, a new job, a sick child, care for an elderly relative? We make a plan, and yet we yield to whatever is the necessity of the day—with cheerfulness! We submit our schedule to the Lord. We know that each day is *still* going according to plan; it's just not necessarily *our* plan.

This came home clearly one wintry day. I had bundled three little ones into the van (no small feat between snow coats and car seats!) to head to the grocery store before noon Mass at the university. We had a Hahn family reunion in Pittsburgh the next day, and I did not yet have the food I was to bring.

I turned the key, and the motor made an odd sound. Urgently, I asked everyone to pray and tried it again to no avail. I was ready to express my exasperation when my five-year-old Gabriel announced, "That's the will of God!" I kept my mouth shut—he was right—and told the children we would go back into the house and regroup.

Once we removed our coats, I surveyed the first floor and realized it was a mess. I quickly negotiated a ride from Scott in a half hour for Mass and marshaled the wee ones to assist in the cleanup.

At Mass we saw a dear friend whom we had not seen in years. Scott asked if he could invite him for lunch. I knew the first floor was clean and that we had enough groceries for lunch, so I was thrilled to say yes. Mid-lunch a call came from my sister-in-law to say that since two of her children had the chicken pox, we would have to postpone the reunion.

God knew that I did not need more groceries, though I thought I did. He also knew that I could offer hospitality more easily if the first floor was clean. And I did not have to go to Confession for venting my anger inappropriately because my son reminded me, "That's the will of God!" Indeed, it was.

Time Wasters

What are ways we waste time? Here is a quick review of nine of them.

First, we may have *unclear goals*. Jesus cautions his disciples,

> For which of you, desiring to build a tower, does not first sit down and count the cost, whether he has enough to complete it? Otherwise, when he has laid a foundation, and is not able to finish, all who see it begin to mock him, saying, "This man began to build, and was not able to finish. (Luke 14:28–30)

We need to count the cost before we begin, plan well, set clear goals and have someone hold us accountable.

Second, we *over schedule.* We set goals that no one but God could accomplish. We over schedule ourselves, or we allow over scheduling of our children's activities. Sometimes we need to take a fresh look at what our schedule should be and adjust it, even if it means declining invitations.

Third, our *lack of planning* dissipates resources of time, energy and finances. Setting a goal without planning how to accomplish it is self-defeating. We cannot even delegate well when help is available, since we did not plan the stages of the project. It is not too late; we can stop mid-project and take time to plan. The temporary stall might be frustrating, but forward progress will quicken once the plan is in effect.

Fourth, *unclear family rules* lead to arguments. Unclear expectations for chores or for privileges with the TV, computer or car build frustrations. If your children do not do a task well, do you redo it, with irritation, rather than training them to improve their skills? Do your rules for privileges include the consequences of infractions? Clear family rules help everyone contribute to both order and peace.

Fifth, a *lack of order* depletes essential time already planned for something else. How often have we searched through stacks of paper for a receipt, a permission slip or an invitation? How often have we been delayed due to mislaid items such as keys, library books, homework, a checkbook or a shoe? If a prayer to Saint Anthony occurs regularly in your home due to lost objects, you might need to go directly to the chapter on home management. (Saint Anthony delights to help us, but he prefers to help us with lost souls more than lost things.) Instead of leaving the house in a frenzy, with many frustrated words said between parents and children, we can contribute to peace through greater order. We need to designate a place for everything and train our family members to help us maintain that order.

Sixth, we can allow irrational fears to lead us to *procrastinate*. "The sluggard says, 'There is a lion in the road! / There is a lion in the streets!'" (Proverbs 26:13). We feel overwhelmed, so we do not do what we can. Or we fear change, so we ignore what can be done today that prepares for that change. "In all toil there is profit, / but mere talk tends only to want" (Proverbs 14:23). If we identify our fears, we may be able to take small steps toward trusting the Lord more.

Seventh, *misplaced priorities* can lead to worthless pursuits that do not merit our time. "He who tills his land will have plenty of bread, / but he who follows worthless pursuits will have plenty of poverty" (Proverbs 28:19). Being busy is not the same as being industrious. One of our misplaced priorities could be perfectionism (which disables us) or never-ending list making (without doing what is on our lists). Another can be others' plans for our time (without asking us first). Once we have established our priorities, then we have a basis for reviewing requests and responding in a way that keeps us on track.

Eighth, *interruptions* can sidetrack us from tasks we do not want to do in the first place; however, all interruptions are not created equal. Prayer and reflection can help us discern. Are the interruptions derailing us (for example, phone calls at the wrong time of day, chunks of time on the Internet or answering e-mails)? Or are they reminding us what our priorities should be (for example, a child who needs a hug, a spouse who needs to talk about the day)? We live what I call an "apostolate of interruption," and God is refining in us a heart of loving service and wisdom to know how to respond to each interruption.

Ninth, *other challenges* may waste time or temporarily demand unusual amounts of time. Those include (but are not limited to) health problems, financial stresses and major life events such as a move, a new job, getting married and having a new baby. We need to learn how to "flex with flux." If we are guided by basic principles that accommodate changes in life's circumstances, we can deal with those challenges without getting knocked off balance.

Whether the goal is to follow a schedule or to deal with time wasters, you want to respond to each person, each task, as if Jesus is asking you, Will you do laundry for me? Will you carpool for me? Will you sew this badge on the Boy Scout shirt for me?

You want your response to be, "Yes, Lord!" As Saint Paul says, "Whatever your task, work heartily, as serving the Lord and not men, knowing that from the Lord you will receive the inheritance as your reward; you are serving the Lord Christ" (Colossians 3:23–24).

Every task can bring us closer to the Lord. This is the difference between being mission-minded and schedule-driven.

CHAPTER NINE

A Mother's Guide to Confirmation

Isaiah prophesies about the gifts of the Spirit that the Messiah will possess: "And the Spirit of the LORD shall rest upon him, / the spirit of wisdom and understanding, the spirit of counsel and might, / the spirit of knowledge and the fear of the LORD" (Isaiah 11:2).

When John the Baptist baptized Jesus, John declared, "I saw the Spirit descend as a dove from heaven and remain on him…. This is he who baptizes with the Holy Spirit" (John 1:32, 33). Jesus is the Messiah; through him the Spirit will be poured out upon all believers, giving them the same gifts.

Through Baptism we receive the gift of the Holy Spirit. Through Confirmation we are sealed with the Holy Spirit, releasing the Spirit's gifts (see *CCC*, 1831). "In him you also, who have heard the word of truth, the gospel of your salvation, and have believed in him, were sealed with the promised Holy Spirit, who is the guarantee of our inheritance until we acquire possession of it, to the praise of his glory" (Ephesians 1:13-14).

These gifts "complete and perfect the virtues of those who receive them. They make the faithful docile in readily obeying divine inspirations" (*CCC*, 1831). Confirmation empowers us to be witnesses through our words and actions, in imitation of Christ, just as the disciples were after they received the Spirit at Pentecost. We are commissioned as soldiers for Christ in the spiritual warfare that rages around us. We receive promptings of the Spirit in our stewardship of relationships and resources.

Jesus used the gifts of the Spirit as he discerned how to spend his time with its human limitations. We need these gifts in managing our time. The first two, wisdom and understanding, help us intellectually discern "the nature of things" (seen and unseen) and morally clarify "the difference of things in their appearance." The next two, counsel and might, help us form "right conclusions" and then "carry them out with energy."[1] The last two, knowledge and fear of the Lord (as well as piety), help us know God and love him reverently, both with a filial fear not to offend him and with a desire to please him. Since we have already received these gifts of the Spirit, we pray for the Lord to release them powerfully in our lives.

Various theologian-saints have connected Isaiah's prophecy not only to Christ but also to individual believers. Saint Augustine "saw in Isaiah's words a complete description of the Holy Spirit's work in the soul."[2] The Holy Spirit *is* at work in our lives. As we grow in Christ, we exercise the gifts the Spirit has given us.

Saint Gregory the Great, building on the teachings of Saint Augustine, understood the gifts of the Spirit "as special aids to the Christian in his war against evil."[3] We are mindful that we are in the midst of spiritual warfare, both with external forces and with our own internal struggles with sin, and yet we are not alone in it. "But rejoice in so far as you share Christ's sufferings, that you may also rejoice and be glad when his glory is revealed. If you are reproached for the name of Christ, you are blessed, because the spirit of glory and of God rests upon you" (1 Peter 4:13–14).

Saint Thomas Aquinas argued that "through the gifts He [the Holy Spirit] moves men as His immediate and direct instruments."[4] Provided there are no obstacles due to sin, we can anticipate insights and inspirations from the Spirit. The question remains, How do we respond to the movement of the Spirit in our lives?

If we focus on the past, especially our failures and sins, we can become distracted. We want to move forward in our spiritual life, and the gifts of the Spirit enable us to embrace the present and anticipate progress in the future. Saint Paul admonishes us, "Look carefully then how you walk, not as unwise men but as wise, making the most of the time, because the days are evil" (Ephesians 5:15–16).

The past has passed; the time for grace is *now!* Let's respond to the grace of this moment with the gifts of the Spirit active in our lives, especially with regard to managing our time.

PART FOUR

*She
provides
tasks
for her
maidens*

CHAPTER TEN

Housework Is God's Work

The Proverbs 31 woman helps everyone's attitude by rising first at the beginning of the day: "She rises while it is yet night / and provides food for her household / and tasks for her maidens" (Proverbs 31:15). She cares for people before she concerns herself—or others—with the day's tasks. Her focus is not simply how they can assist her but rather how she can also meet their needs, including her oversight of their work.

In humility she utilizes others' help. She knows her limitations as well as how much more can be accomplished with the assistance of others. As my dear friend Roseanne said recently, "I tell all young mothers: Accept all help you are offered!"

The Proverbs 31 woman provides structure not only for her tasks but also for those of her household, bringing order to her home. "Like the sun rising in the heights of the LORD, / so is the beauty of a good wife in her well-ordered home" (Sirach 26:16). Let's examine housework as God's work and briefly look at parallels between cleaning and the sacrament of Confession.

THE GENIUS OF WOMAN

John Paul the Great attributed a woman's emphasis on the human person in relationships to what he called "the genius of woman":

Perhaps more than men, women *acknowledge the person,* because they see persons with their hearts. They see them independently of various ideological or political systems. They see others in their greatness and limitations; they try to go out to them and *help them.* In this way the basic plan of the Creator takes flesh in the history of humanity and there is constantly revealed, in the variety of vocations, that *beauty*—not merely physical, but above all spiritual— which God bestowed from the very beginning on all, and in a particular way on women.[1]

Women enable persons to reach their potential by focusing on their dignity and worth.

A man tends to describe himself initially in terms of his career, "I am a professor," or, "I am an accountant." A woman, on the other hand, seems to respond first in terms of relationships, "I am a wife," or, "I am a mom." A woman's roles, in relation to someone else, include daughter of God, daughter, daughter-in-law, wife, mother, sister, sister-in-law, granddaughter, grandmother, niece, aunt, godmother and so on. Even homemaking tasks are not primarily about the house or the things she has collected but about making a special place for the persons who dwell there.

A DWELLING PLACE

God's presence is our dwelling place. As the psalmist writes, "LORD, you have been our dwelling place / in all generations" (Psalm 90:1). Heaven is our eternal home because *he* is there.

The Lord called creation into existence as a temporary home for us. The Spirit hovered over creation to bring order out of chaos: "In the beginning God created the heavens and the earth. Now the earth was a formless void, there was darkness over the deep, and God's spirit hovered over the water" (Genesis 1:1–2, *JB*).

The Hebrew word for *hover* is used elsewhere in Scripture to describe a mother bird hovering over her nest, caring for the needs of her young. Like the Holy Spirit, hovering over the darkness and formless abyss to bring order and beauty out of chaos, so we hover over the drawers, closets, cupboards and counters to bring order out of chaos.

The question remains, how do you hover? Do you hover like the nurturing mother bird hovering over her brood or like a looming drill sergeant issuing orders? Even good things done without love are meaningless, according to 1 Corinthians 13. To paraphrase, you can have the best plan for home organization, but if you do not have love, it counts for nothing. Love has to be at the heart of everything you do.

KEEPER OF THE HOME

Saint Paul commands the older women to train the younger women how to love their husbands and children and how to be domestic as part of their Christian witness (see Titus 2:3–5). *Domestic* can be translated "keepers at home."[2] What does it mean to be a keeper?

If we return to the Garden of Eden, some of the instructions God gave Adam included tilling and keeping the garden (see Genesis 2:15). Adam was to "keep" or "guard" the garden. More than simply looking after the garden, Adam was to guard the garden from the presence of evil, thus protecting himself and eventually Eve.

Throughout the Old Testament there are numerous references to people whose task was to be a "keeper" of various areas: keeper of the field (Jeremiah 4:17), keeper of the walls (Song of Solomon 5:7), keeper of the entry (1 Chronicles 9:19), keeper of the gates to the tabernacle (1 Chronicles 9:19), keeper of the prison (Genesis 39:21), keeper of a sheepfold (1 Samuel 17: 20), keeper of the wardrobe (2 Kings 22:14), keeper of the king's forest (Nehemiah 2:8), keeper of the east gate (Nehemiah 3:29), keeper of the harem (see Esther 2:3), keeper of the vineyards (Song of Solomon 1:6), keepers of the watch (2 Kings 11:5) and keeper of the door (Jeremiah 35:4). Keepers exercised authority in protecting others. They were to guard the precious treasures within.

The psalmist describes the Lord as our keeper:

> The LORD is your keeper;
> > the LORD is your shade
> > on your right hand.
> The sun shall not strike you by day,
> > nor the moon by night.
>
> The LORD will keep you from all evil;
> > he will keep your life.
> The LORD will keep
> > your going out and your coming in
> > from this time forth and for evermore. (Psalm 121:5–8)

The Lord protects us from harm. He guards us because we are his precious treasures.

He is the one who has called us to be house *keepers*. We are to be watchful of those who enter, protective of those within and aware that we are stewards of our home.

HOMEMAKING IN IMITATION OF GOD

It is important to keep a sense of humor in the midst of doing something as serious as the vocation of marriage. Recently a Web site posted the following anecdotes regarding homemaking:

- Does a clean house indicate that there is a broken computer in it?
- Why do people keep running over a string a dozen times with their vacuum cleaner, then reach down, pick it up, examine it, then put it down to give the vacuum one more chance?
- How do those dead bugs get into those closed light fixtures?[3]

Besides humor, we have a reservoir of grace available to us, not just for spiritual tasks but for everything we do. We can confidently approach Jesus for the grace and wisdom we need to be keepers of our homes.

> For we have not a high priest who is unable to sympathize with our weaknesses, but one who in every respect has been tempted as we are, yet without sinning. Let us then with confidence draw near to the throne of grace, that we may receive mercy and find grace to help in time of need. (Hebrews 4:15–16)

Jesus understands our challenges. He invites us to make a home with him: "If a man loves me, he will keep my word, and my Father will love him, and we will come to him and make our home with him" (John 14:23). He wants to make a home with us, where we love and obey him.

MENIAL WORK CAN BE MEANINGFUL WORK

We want our home to be his home. That means we have to remember the One for whom we work—the Lord. As Holly Pierlot reflects, "Jesus was asking for the dedication of my entire self to my vocation."[4] Each task becomes a response to the Lord. *He* is the one asking me to cook dinner, do laundry, find a Band-Aid, pick up a tearful baby, sweep up the crumbs. Moving away from self-pity ("No one notices all I am doing. I am merely the unpaid maid of the house!") and toward imitating Christ's selfless love, we recall for whom we do each task. As the Franciscan University rugby team proclaims, "We play for an audience of One!" So do we.

Saint Thérèse of Lisieux, Saint Faustina and Mother Teresa of Calcutta are all renowned for urging us not to focus on doing great things for God as much as small things for God with great love. We are all capable of doing that. Despising small things leads to failure, little by little (see Sirach 19:1). However, when we do not despise small beginnings, we succeed little by little. We want to rise above the menial to see the meaning-filled picture with each task.

WHY DO MOMS ALWAYS GET THE TRASH?

Have you noticed that moms always get the trash? My children reach around my husband to hand trash to me; even Scott hands me trash. This is not just a phenomenon in American culture. A Nigerian priest told me that in his village, there is no word for "mother" but rather a phrase, *O ba' taan*, which means "woman who cleans dirt." And there is no word for "Mary" but rather a phrase, *O ba' taan pa,* which means "Great woman who cleans dirt."

Many household tasks involve cleaning. We wipe faces, noses, fingers and bottoms. We scour kitchen counters and scrub bathroom toilets and shower stalls. We wash floors and walls. We clean clothes and dishes.

Since cleaning plays such a role in housework, I examined Scriptures that mentioned cleaning. I was surprised to find no use of "cleaning" applied to ordinary housework; instead it involved setting apart common objects for sacred liturgical use.

The Israelites cleansed the altar (Exodus 29:36), women (Leviticus 12:8), clothing (Leviticus 13:6), homes (Leviticus 14:49), men for priestly service (Numbers 8:6), the house of the Lord (2 Chronicles 29:15–16), vessels for use in the house of the Lord (Isaiah 66:20), the land (Ezekiel 39:12, 14, 16) and the sanctuary (Ezekiel 45:18). These were ordinary people or objects set apart for extraordinary use. (In a similar way, water is blessed, and then as holy water it is used to bless our homes, our children and our belongings to set them apart for God.)

Even more important, God's people need to be cleansed from sin. A number of Old Testament passages refer to this, including the description of the Day of Atonement: "For on this day shall atonement be made for you, to cleanse you; from all your sins you shall be clean before the LORD" (Leviticus 16:30).

The New Testament has many references to being cleansed from sin. For example, Saint John writes, "But if we walk in the light, as he is in the light, we have fellowship with one another, and the blood of Jesus his Son cleanses us from all sin" (1 John 1:7). Through the forgiveness of sins, having been washed in the waters of Baptism, we are made holy for the Lord, set apart for him. The Lord delights to make us clean, and he calls us to imitate him: collecting the trash, removing dirt and helping reconcile relationships in our homes. Through our ordinary work God's extraordinary grace is at work in us.

HOME IS A PLACE OF ORDER

Whether a woman is single or married, with or without children, regardless of her residence—a dorm room, rental apartment, a trailer or a house—there is something within her that longs to create a nest, a home. Franciscan University uses identical furniture in each dorm room, but if you go from room to room in the women's dorms, you will be amazed to see how many arrangements can be made, with many added personal touches, to make it homey. I think that the impulse for a woman to create a home is God-given. (For a concise sheet to use as you consider purchasing a home, I have developed a form. See Appendix C: Key Questions for Buying Your Next Home.)

Jesus has prepared a home for us in heaven, just as we prepare a place for each of our loved ones in our home. We want to cultivate a sense of belonging, assuring them that we have thought about them. Jesus told his disciples, "In my Father's house are many rooms; if it were not so, would I have told you that I go to prepare a place for you? And when I go and prepare a place for you, I will come again and will take you to myself, that where I am you may be also" (John 14:2–3).

How do we prepare a room for someone? I have drafted an appendix of critical questions for room organization that helps me transform a room into a space that is both useful and beautiful.⁵ (See Appendix D: Making a House a Home, Room by Room.) You dream about the function of the space; then you structure it to fulfill that purpose. You keep whatever works well; you change those things that do not. Here is the seven-step process I follow.

First, are major changes needed, such as moving a wall, changing flooring, adding a drop ceiling, changing doors or windows? Is there adequate light? Are there enough outlets? You can feel locked into difficulties in the structure of a room that actually can be changed, though perhaps not without a good carpenter or electrician. To help you dream, sketch the primary elements of the room (including measurements), noting unusual features.

Second, are there cosmetic changes that could alter the mood of the room? A fresh coat of paint or plasterwork can brighten a room or make it seem larger or more intimate. Deep-cleaning the carpet or adding quarter-round moulding might improve the floor's appearance. Or perhaps the flooring needs to be changed to easy-to-clean tile or linoleum, new hardwood laminate or carpet. Dressing the walls with a border or wallpaper, adding a chair rail or decorative wood trim around windows or doorways, or changing curtains can give a room a facelift quickly.

Third, is the furniture appropriate for the purpose of the room? Is it arranged in the most helpful way, with easy access and walkways around large pieces? Is there too much in the room? Are the pieces too large for the room, or is a critical piece missing that would make the room more versatile? Is any furniture in need of repair, a fresh coat of paint or perhaps an updated look with new hardware? Is another bookshelf, closet organizer or trash can needed?

Fourth, what about storage needs? For a room to function well, objects related to its purpose need a place in closets, drawers, organizers, baskets, a desk or on shelves. Will materials related to the function of the room fit in these containers to maximize a sense of order and beauty? The tried-and-true saying applies: a place for everything and everything in its place. You need to envision this before you can make it a reality.

Fifth, you cannot revamp your entire home next week. What is a realistic time frame for tackling one room? Perhaps you can commit to one area each day or one hour per day, until you are done. One professional organizer suggests that you try to fill two garbage bags a day: one for trash and one for giving away. In six days you will have sorted twelve bags of stuff. And make no new purchases until everything you already have is organized, given away or thrown out. You organize one drawer at a time, one closet at a time, one room at a time, one floor at a time. It may be slow, but change will happen, and everyone in the family will be grateful. To help yourself persevere, ask yourself, *what will give me a feeling of success?*

When we moved to Joliet, Illinois, Scott was mid-semester in his first teaching position, and we had three little ones who were four years old, three years old and five weeks old. Scott was doing all he could not to drown in the details of being a college professor for the first time. I was on my own to unpack and settle, except for his library.

Our dining room had the fewest number of things that had to be put away. Since it was already beautifully decorated by the former owners, I decided to unpack that room first (after essentials for living). I would stand in the doorway with my hands shielding my view so that all I could see was this beautiful, ordered room. What a mental lift it was! I would tell myself that soon my whole house would look like this. It took about six weeks, unpacking at least one box a night. It was not easy having chaos for that long, but order in our home became more of a reality every day.

Sixth, is there temporary storage where you can place boxes, so that you can make progress more quickly? As you work through a room, use several boxes for sorting things that do not belong in this space, labeled as follows: "Belongs elsewhere," "Give away," "Throw away," "Repair" and "Return" (items that belong in other people's homes).

Do not get sidetracked by what is in the boxes—keep working on that room until you are done. Use a pad to note potentially distracting thoughts. For instance, if you are organizing a closet and realize that nail holes need to be filled, jot that down for a later time when you will fill all the nail holes in all of the rooms on one floor of the house. When time is limited, you need to stay on task.

Seventh (and last), move into this room items you have had elsewhere in your home that follow the function of this room. Julie Morgenstern, in her book *Organizing from the Inside Out,* uses the example of how a kindergarten room is set up: There are zones in the room for various purposes, and the materials needed for each purpose are also located there.[6] This helps everyone maintain order. Once you have things in place, explain to your family why they fit the room's function, and your family will help you maintain the new order.

Many people do not feel that they were born organized, but that does not mean that it is not possible to become organized. This is a learned skill. For extra help you may hire someone, as long as the person understands that you want him or her to train you to organize instead of doing it for you. Extra help is available through a Web site managed by Sandra Felton, author of many good books on organization.[7]

MAINTAIN THE SPACE

Clutter management. There is a difference between a dirty room and one that is cluttered, though both put limits on the use of the space. What routines do you need to keep rooms orderly? Enlist the whole family to limit clutter in common areas. Also require them to maintain their bedrooms. Then everyone enjoys the order you have established.

Family management. What basic rules will govern the family for maintaining the space? For instance: If you pick it up, you put it down. If you put it down, you pick it up. If you get it out, you put it away. If you make a mess, you clean the mess. And if you fix anything to eat, you put away the ingredients, preferably before you sit down to eat. (Obviously, young ones are rather limited in which rules they can follow, but older children and all adults can comply.)

Once you set new rules, help your family establish new habits by holding them accountable. For instance, I may ask, "Is there a reason I found a plate of raisins on the TV?" Apart from the possibility that it is a unique science experiment for class—show me the paperwork!—the correct answer is, "No; I'll take it right away to the kitchen, Mom."

Cleaning management. As you manage clutter, you simplify the cleaning process, but cleaning still must be done. The best book for cleaning organization that I have read is called *Sidetracked Home Executives: From Pigpen to Paradise,* written by two sisters, Pam Young and Peggy Jones. I read this book during a night of labor with my firstborn, and if a book is funny during labor, it is a good read! These sisters were more disorganized than anything I imagined possible, and they found a way, working together, to bring order out of their chaos.

These easily sidetracked homemakers have given many people hope. One of their mottos is "We Change Lives With 3 x 5s!"[8] They list all possible jobs for cleaning any room in the house (in the back of their book) in terms of daily, weekly, biweekly, monthly and seasonal chores.

For each room they recommend that you list one task per note card, color-coded based on frequency: blue for daily or every-other-day jobs, white for weekly or biweekly jobs, yellow for monthly tasks, orange for seasonal jobs, red for holiday tasks, pink for personal tasks. Twenty-five years ago I could not afford colored note cards, so I cut construction paper to the size of index cards and created the same system. Today you can download the information you want, customize it for your home and print cards for yourself. [9]

Once each task is listed separately, time the jobs and designate any task as a mini-job if it takes less than ten minutes—*many* tasks are five-minute (or less) jobs. Determine a time each day by which you will complete the daily jobs. When you are ready to begin, closely follow the cleaning routine that you have set up, noting challenges. The second week, only make slight adjustments—you are working on a new habit. The third week, evaluate and fine-tune only.

The seasonal cards include garden, yard, garage and shed jobs. Many home maintenance tasks are difficult to remember, such as cleaning furnace filters or replacing throwaway filters, draining hose lines before the first frost, checking bathroom grout, fixing broken screens, scheduling lawnmower tune-ups before spring and checking the Freon supply in an air-conditioning unit before summer heat arrives. If you record the tasks on seasonal cards, the reminders will be waiting for you, filed under the correct month.

Personal cards can be reminders for dental and medical checkups, thank-you notes to be sent, financial due dates and periodic obligations. Holiday cards include special tasks related to gifts, cards, decorating and special baking. Cards can remind you to prepare for Advent, Lent (for example, buying candles for an Advent wreath before Advent begins) and other liturgical celebrations.

If your children (or someone you hired) help you clean, add instructions to the cards, so they know how to do each task. Either designate who should do the chores and when, or shuffle the cards and have the children draw one. Include on the card what supplies are needed to complete that chore, and store those supplies near the point of use. It may not save you money on supplies—unless you find them on sale—but why not at least save time by having cleaning supplies located in each bathroom, for instance, or in a designated closet on each floor?

The *Sidetracked Home Executives* system helped me take the huge job of cleaning the house and break it into incremental steps. It also helped me make better use of offers of help. As we moved from an apartment to a house, I adapted the system, reused many cards and added more for additional rooms.

When I was off my feet for weeks due to bleeding during my pregnancy with Gabriel, I was helped by a friend, Sally, who later became my sister-in-law, and a high school girl from church. I could give them cards for the jobs that needed to be done. Even after I was able to be up and about, the student still came over to help me. She would walk in and ask, "Where are my cards for today?" She would work her way through the cards and then hand them back to me to file. It was such a blessing.

HOME IS A PLACE OF BEAUTY

More than function, beauty in our homes ministers to our souls. Beauty communicates peace; it creates a kind of sanctuary.

> One thing have I asked of the LORD,
>   that will I seek after;
> that I may dwell in the house of the LORD
>   all the days of my life,
> to behold the beauty of the LORD,
>   and to inquire in his temple. (Psalm 27:4)

Beauty reflects God. When we witness a magnificent sunset or sunrise, view mountains rising majestically against the clear blue Colorado sky or watch the variations of sea foam on the ocean's waves, our hearts are lifted toward the Lord. Great art in our homes has a similar effect.

Home is a place where each person is nurtured, in part through the beauty we create there. In Ezra we read "Blessed be the LORD, the God of our fathers, who put such a thing as this into the heart of the king, to beautify the house of the LORD which is in Jerusalem" (Ezra 7:27). Just as the king wanted to make the Lord's house beautiful to reflect the Lord's beauty, so we want to make our homes beautiful so that they reflect the beauty and dignity of each person who resides there.

"He has made everything beautiful in its time" (Ecclesiastes 3:11). God can help us work within our means to bring more beauty to our home; it is not about expense. We can paint bedrooms with soothing colors or use colors that stimulate appetite in the dining room or kitchen. We can look for attractive fabrics, rich in texture and color, for curtains, recovering furniture or accent pillows. We can discover our style of decorating (classic, romantic, modern or eclectic). We can add a crucifix above a door, frame artwork for a particular space or make collections of family photos around the house. However we decorate, we want the beauty of our home to draw our hearts to each other and to the Lord.

> By wisdom a house is built,
>   and by understanding it is established;
> by knowledge the rooms are filled
>   with all precious and pleasant riches. (Proverbs 24:3–4)

We are not talking about a museum. Wisdom reveals how to have a beautiful house that is a real home. That means we have to practice detachment at the same time we provide and maintain beautiful things in our home. We remind ourselves that people are always more important than things.

As our children became teens, we wanted an addition on our home that could be a gathering place for our children and their friends. Our new family room was in pristine condition when our son's youth group came for the evening. After they left I noticed indelible marker marks on the new built-in computer table. If I had wanted things to remain perfect, I could never share them. I wanted to live by principles I had taught my children their whole lives, "Jesus gives to you *so that* you can share with others."

This became clearer than ever a few years later. We had moved into a new home and had just refinished our eighty-year-old kitchen floor, made of soft pine. We welcomed a group of college women who wanted to hold a fundraiser for their retreat. After they left my husband urged me to look at the kitchen floor; something was wrong. As I walked into the kitchen, I noticed small circles on the floor. I knelt for a closer look and realized, to my horror, that there were hundreds of small indentations—holes—in our newly refinished floor. One of the women in stiletto heels had pierced the floor, leaving hundreds of holes.

The refinisher returned to examine the floor. He could not sand it down far enough to get rid of the holes without ruining the floor. He said we could cover the floor with linoleum, replace the wood floor with a new wood floor or live with the floor as it was. We decided to live with it.

Then we realized that we still had a choice: Would we lament that we had opened our home to all of these people, or would we look at the floor as a reminder of the wonderful college women who had blessed so many people through their fundraising event in our home?

After all, our possessions were not ours to keep to ourselves. We were to be generous, because the house belonged to God, the things belonged to God, and the people belonged to God. "To cling to things is to feed avarice,"[10] but to detach from things in a spirit of generosity is to reflect the image of our heavenly Father.

We chose to thank God for the event. Recently someone actually complimented the great job we did "distressing" the floor. We had to laugh—the stress part of the distressing situation was now leading to compliments on our antique floor!

HOME IS A PLACE OF SAFETY AND PEACE

When the people of Israel were on the brink of entering the Promised Land, Moses could not lead them in. He was allowed to climb a mountain to at least see the Promised Land before he died. So before he went, he shared this important thought: "The eternal God is your dwelling place, / and underneath are the everlasting arms" (Deuteronomy 33:27).

Moses reassured God's people, "You are in a place of uncertainty, but God is the One in whom you must trust; he is your refuge. He has brought you this far, and though I cannot lead you to your new home, he will bring you in safely. You are getting a new home, but never forget, *God* is your dwelling place."

Many years later King David proclaimed this same truth. Though he was on the run from King Saul, who was seeking to kill him, he declared,

> ...You are my refuge,
>   a strong tower against the enemy.

> Let me dwell in your tent for ever!
>> Oh, to be safe under the shelter of your wings!
>> (Psalm 61:3, 4)

God is *our* refuge, and he enables us to make our homes a refuge too.

We can create a safe haven to welcome the family back from the storms of life. We can contribute to peace in our homes through conflict resolution.[11] We want to communicate respect in our conversations, even with young children. We choose to believe the best of each other, knowing that we tend to notice others' sins more clearly than our own. We can resolve disagreements as lovingly—and quickly—as possible. We do not indulge in the luxury of grudges; true forgiveness brings peace to our home. When things bother us, we find the polite way to discuss it, keeping Christ between us: acknowledging his presence, remaining prayerful, seeking to understand instead of simply being understood and weighing our words knowing that Christ knows all things. We facilitate a sense of peace by contributing to reconciliation within our home.

Keep short accounts

Does your home feel peaceful? Something as simple as lamplight, candlelight or a lit fireplace can communicate warmth and comfort more than harsh overhead lights. (Lower wattage use saves on energy bills too.) Playing soft classical or religious music can limit noise. Using a phone system that includes an intercom can cut down on yelling to get each other's attention.

The greatest sense of peace will come from living our faith well. When the Prince of Peace rules in our hearts, he reigns in our homes.

CHAPTER ELEVEN

The Value of Homemaking

D o you feel competent in homemaking? Most young women today prepare more for careers, which they might never have, than for homemaking, which many will choose. Schools rarely offer home economics, unless it is a vocational school for students who will not attend college.

PREPARATION FOR MANAGING A HOME

Throughout our engagement my mom and dad would remind Scott and me to prepare more for marriage than for our wedding day. Why? As significant a feast day as our wedding day would be, we needed to prepare more for our life together. That included, among other things, my preparation for doing the work of housework.

This wisdom was driven home by a comment from a friend, the only child of a well-to-do couple, who had not followed this advice. The bride's approach to the wedding had been to make it a spare-no-expense extravaganza, though the financial circumstances of her beloved were meager at best. Later, following a bridal shower for me, she spoke with a sadness that clearly colored her outlook on life: "I awoke two days after our wedding to realize that I'm going to clean toilets for the rest of my life!"

When we think about the years that we devote to homemaking, is it not amazing that so little training is offered?

Rather than complaining about what we did not get, we should be thankful for all the ways we have become competent in other areas, because that has built our confidence that we can learn whatever we need to know. After all, how do we grow in competence in any skill? We learn from good teachers and helpful materials. The same principles apply here, for no one is born a good cook or a good cleaner.

Older Women as Mentors

We need knowledge and skill to accomplish the tasks before us. If we have a teachable spirit, we will get the help we need. God has provided a rich resource of wisdom for us through older women who have already lived through our season of life. Saint Paul admonished Titus to instruct the older women of their responsibility in this:

> Bid the older women likewise to be reverent in behavior, not to be slanderers or slaves to drink; they are to teach what is good, and so train the young women to love their husbands and children, to be sensible, chaste, domestic, kind, and submissive to their husbands, that the word of God may not be discredited. (Titus 2:3–5)

Two things are needed: older women willing to teach; younger women willing to learn. And though this relates to our hidden life, it is part of our public testimony, for the goal is not to discredit the Word of God. We pray for the courage and humility to pursue competence and even excellence in these areas.

Another translation of *domestic* in this verse is "busy at home."[1] Homemakers are not women who waste hours watching soap operas and eating bonbons. They are women who hone skills, learn homemaking hobbies, develop home businesses and apply stewardship to their time, finances and other resources. They are busy doing good (see Proverbs 31:12).

One of the deepest desires of my heart for this Proverbs 31 study is to generate meaningful intergenerational conversations about the wisdom we need for our vocation of marriage. We want to take advantage of all that the older women have learned. For those of us who are the bridge between newly-weds and great-grandmothers, we want to continue to learn while we share our lived wisdom. We need a clear signal from younger women that they are willing to be taught.

RESOURCES AND TOOLS

If there are no mentors available, there are other sources of wisdom for you. Ask relatives or friends to recommend books or videos on some aspect of homemaking. You can borrow their copies, check them out of the library or purchase them.

New materials are being written for women who struggle with Attention Deficit Disorder (ADD) or Attention Deficit and Hyperactivity Disorder (ADHD).[2] In the past most of the research on these disorders has been done on school-age children, primarily boys, but more and more adults are being studied. Finally resources are available to guide women (and men) with ADD and ADHD, so that they understand how to work with their disability, especially in the area of organization. This can make an enormous difference in a woman's ability to bring order to her home.

Another critical question is, do we have the tools to do our tasks quickly and efficiently? If we were professional cleaners, would we use the tools we currently have, such as ripped rags, worn-out mops or a broom that is losing its bristles? We shortchange ourselves if we do not have quality tools. We would save time and perhaps eventually save money, as well as do a better job, with the right tools. Perhaps we should offer a tool shower for a bride-to-be, with every woman bringing something she has found indispensable in her homemaking.

I struggled when I had to use wedding money to purchase a vacuum cleaner! I could not believe that I had to fork out money for one, but after borrowing the neighbor's each week for three months, I purchased the cheapest one I could find. And it did the job I paid for it to do—poorly—until years later, when we purchased a good vacuum cleaner.

THE COST OF DISORGANIZATION

We need to evaluate the cost of our disorganization. Disorder breeds disorder. Are we willing to continue a haphazard approach to home management because we think we lack the time and resources to be organized? Or do we see the value of investing time and resources now for great benefits in the long run?

Order encourages more order. The more we contribute to an orderly and beautiful home, the more our spouse and children will want to maintain it. When the children enter the kitchen with a shiny sink or a cleaned-off counter, they are more inclined to help it stay that way. And if they leave it a mess, we can train them to return it to the order in which they found it. We have already shown them how it can and should look.

If we cooperate with grace, we can also learn from our flaws, failings and fears. We humble ourselves to ask for help, and we thank God for all we have learned. We are in the process of becoming good homemakers—we have not arrived at perfection yet.

A wonderful Web site that has helped thousands of families is FlyLady.net.[3] FlyLady and her crew target a different area of the home each week, one task per day, to move forward the organization of that space. Their lighthearted humor is an encouragement to take the task more seriously and to take ourselves less seriously.

✳ HOW HAVE I VIEWED HOMEMAKING?

Based on a renewed vision for what homemaking entails, do you need to adjust your perspective? After a number of conversations with college women, I have found that it is important to clarify what home is *not*.

Home is not a pit stop where we quickly change clothes and refuel so that we can begin the next important lap of our race through the day. Instead, home is the place where we welcome each family member with a sense of belonging.

Home is not a prison where we lose our freedom; rather, home is the place where we are free to bring the fullness of our womanhood to bear in every sphere of life.

Home is not "a woman's place," as if she were a dog chained to a doghouse. A woman's place is in the heart—the heart of her husband, the heart of her children and the heart of her home.

Home is not a cage where we are trapped. Instead, home is a refuge that we create for every family member.

Homemaking is not a waste of our time, talents or intelligence. Homemaking is a call to express fully our personhood and thereby enable every member of the family to understand his or her dignity and worth.

I am not the unpaid maid. I am the queen of the realm, the heart of my home.

THE VALUE OF A HIDDEN LIFE

Consider the value of the "hidden" life of Mary. Mary was the wife of Saint Joseph and the mother of one child, Jesus. She did not do anything our culture would recognize as significant; she was "just" a homemaker. However, Mary's life was rich; it was full. (Can you imagine her dropping Jesus off at day care so she could do something "important"?)

Jesus chose to live thirty of his thirty-three years on earth with Mary, at home, and many of those years would have included Saint Joseph. We know that Saint Joseph was with Mary when Jesus, at age twelve, lingered in the temple for three days. We know that Saint Joseph was not at the foot of the cross with Mary—the only place Jesus' father would be if he were alive. After Saint Joseph died, Jesus would have provided for Mary with his carpentry skills.

Think of all that Jesus could have accomplished during those years he spent with Mary. But it seems that the most valuable use of his time during those years was to be at home. Was this worthwhile? Saint Josemaría Escrivá writes, "The world admires only the spectacular sacrifice, because it does not realize the value of the sacrifice that is hidden and silent."[4]

Being needed is more important than being noticed. Value the time you have in your "hidden life," regardless of whether or not your family notices your sacrifices. Your toddler does not greet you in the morning with, "Thanks for changing my diaper, Mom!" Your baby does not say, "Thanks for waking up with me throughout the night!" Even your husband may not notice the many little ways you love the family throughout the day. But you are walking the path of Jesus with Mary in a hidden life, and it is rich with value.

DOES YOUR FAMILY VALUE YOUR HOMEMAKING?

There is a complementarity with your spouse: He provides for the family through his work outside the home; you provide for the family through your work within the home. Both support and encourage each other. Both provide for the essential needs of the family; each strengthens the other through service. He is free to work on his career because you are holding down the home front; you are free to work at home because he is working outside of the home.[5]

Increasing numbers of young men are doing the math and figuring out what a dual-income couple could earn. They are not even preparing themselves mentally, let alone financially, to support a wife, so that she is free to care for the family at home.

One critical question remains, does your husband value your work at home? In terms of homemaking, what did your husband's mother do that he hopes you will imitate? What did his mother do that he does not want you to do? Likewise, what do you want to imitate from key women in your life? And what example do you not want to follow?

How does your husband's attitude set the tone for the children's attitude about your work in the home? Even with his support, your children can be influenced by pressures they feel outside the home about your "lack" of a career.

My sister Kari and I met at our parents' home in Cincinnati, Ohio, with our young children. We still had siblings at home, one of whom was a brother in grade school. Mom told us that he had informed her that she needed to get a job. She was the only mother in the classroom who stayed at home all day and did not work! Apparently he found it embarrassing.

We were ready to read him the riot act, but Mom said, "Don't worry about it. I'm not going to get a job. I told him I already have one: caring for your dad and you! He'll get a little older, and then he'll appreciate my ministry of presence."

"Tasks for Maidens" Means Teamwork

The Proverbs 31 woman does not work alone. Verse 15 refers to tasks she readies for her maidens, the women who assist her. Who helps you accomplish the work of housework?

Children are your homegrown team! They are eager to work alongside you, especially if you can make it fun. When my two sisters and I were expecting babies at the same time, our youngest sister, Kristi, lamented that she only had a two-year-old to help her, while Kari and I both had children ten and older. "You have so much help from your kids!"

I smiled and simply said, "Kristi, we grew it! We once were where you are. And even your two-year-old will be more helpful than you can imagine."

How can you help your children assist you? You can create chore charts for them and post them at the point of use. This limits your nagging and increases their accountability. Pairing certain chores with mealtimes is helpful, since it is a natural break from other tasks. Train your children; it takes more time initially but really pays off later.

We have machines that help us—dishwashers, washers and dryers, vacuum cleaners, sewing machines and so on. Two hundred years ago women did not dream of having the kind of help that is now at our fingertips. At the same time, machines have also increased work by increasing expectations. We do laundry more often, and we have more clothes to launder than in past centuries.

We can hire people to help us, as humbling as that might be. We need a plan so that our organization helps them to help us. We need to delegate well as good stewards of their precious time and our limited funds. Clear expectations, good explanations, accountability and review are essential for a good working relationship with a worker. Again, it may take longer initially to train hired help, but it pays off in the long run as tasks are done the way we want them done. We have to demonstrate how we want things done, so that we do not have to refold the clothes, dust the room again or reload the dishwasher after they leave.

The Proverbs 31 woman works diligently and accepts the help that is available. If we follow her example, we will walk the path of wisdom, tackling the tasks of homemaking with a desire to serve the Lord and utilizing willing workers who assist us.

CHAPTER TWELVE

A Mother's Guide to Confession

Baptism takes care of original sin and all actual sin committed up to that point. But what about sins committed after Baptism?

Saint John admonishes us to deal forthrightly with our sin: "If we say we have no sin, we deceive ourselves, and the truth is not in us. If we confess our sins, he is faithful and just, and will forgive our sins and cleanse us from all unrighteousness" (1 John 1:8, 9).

God's faithfulness draws us to him; his forgiveness restores us.

Saint James indicates that the procedure for healing involves approaching the "elders" or "priests" (in Greek, *presbuterois*) of the Church for Confession and anointing with oil. "Therefore confess your sins to one another, and pray for one another, that you may be healed. The prayer of a righteous man has great power in its effects" (James 5:16).

Frequently the question is asked, *why confess to a priest when we can apologize for our sins directly to Jesus?* We can and should daily confess our sins to Jesus, using an examination of conscience and making an act of contrition. However, we recognize that as sorry as we are for our sins, we lack perfect contrition. We have mixed motives, as do our young children, who sometimes have remorse for getting caught rather than true repentance. In the sacrament of Confession, the

Spirit perfects our contrition, as long as we have a firm purpose of amendment, a sincere intention of not committing the sins again. The Lord forgives us through the priest's words of absolution.

There is also a corporate consequence to our sins. We recognize that our sins not only damage our relationship with the Lord but also harm the body of Christ. By God's grace he allows us, through penance, to help repair the damage caused by our sins.

This is an example of how well God fathers us. We see it clearly when we apply it to the discipline of children. If a boy who was angry with his father spray-painted terrible things about his dad on a building, he would have two steps to take in restoring his relationship with his father. First, he would need to apologize for what he had done and ask for forgiveness. Second, he would need to repair the damage he had caused. Through Confession the Lord forgives us, and through penance he enables us to restore some strength to the body of Christ, which we have weakened through our sins.

In preparation for celebrating the Passover, it was the Hebrew homemaker's task to rid the house of leaven completely. This was an important task, with serious consequences if it was not done carefully: "Seven days you shall eat unleavened bread; on the first day you shall put away leaven out of your houses, for if any one eats what is leavened, from the first day until the seventh day, that person shall be cut off from Israel" (Exodus 12:15).

In preparing to receive Christ, our Paschal Lamb, Saint Paul commands, "Let us, therefore, celebrate the festival, not with the old leaven, the leaven of malice and evil, but with the unleavened bread of sincerity and truth" (1 Corinthians 5:8). How much more important is it that we eradicate sin from our lives than eliminate leaven from our homes?

In preparation for receiving our Lord at Easter, commonly referred to as our Easter duty, the *Catechism* teaches, "According to the Church's command, 'after having attained the age of discretion, each of the faithful is bound by an obligation faithfully to confess serious sins at least once a year'" ([Cf. CIC, can. 989; Council of Trent (1551): DS 1683; DS 1708], *CCC*, 1457). If Confession is a lot like a bath, think how it would be for ourselves and others if we only bathed once a year! For the good of those around us, as well as for our soul's sake, we do not want to settle for the bare minimum.

If we are aware that we have committed a mortal sin, we need to go to Confession as soon as possible. A mortal sin involves a grave or serious matter, our knowledge that it was wrong before we committed the sin and our deliberate consent to commit the sin. At the same time, we acknowledge that the path to mortal sins is often beaten down by habits of venial sins. We do not want *any* sins to weaken our relationship with the Lord. Sins are more than broken laws—they lead to broken hearts and shattered lives.

As homemakers, we play a crucial role in encouraging family members to get to Confession. We take good care of our children's bodies, insisting on regular bathing. Why would we not take care of our children's souls and schedule regular Confession? Instead of thinking about the inconvenience to our schedule or the cost of the gas to drive our children to Confession, we need to focus on how much all of us will benefit when any of us receives this sacrament. This is an answer to prayer for our teens who are feeling inundated with peer pressure and the immorality of our culture, coping with hormone shifts and related passions and struggling with living in a way that pleases the Lord.

One of my heart's desires has been that our children develop a habit of going to Confession as teens. Not only does it provide a safeguard—knowing they will go to Confession helps them resist some temptations—but it also gives them a solid foundation for adulthood. I believe that this will bless our future in-laws and grandchildren immeasurably.

We face challenges in choosing to go to Confession. One is our ability to deceive ourselves by downplaying our faults and blaming others. We need an honest assessment of our culpability. Another is our judgment in comparing ourselves to others and thinking we are better than most. But we need to compare ourselves to Jesus. When we look at our holiness compared to his, we know how much we need the grace of the sacrament.

Finally, we are challenged by our concupiscence, or the tendency to sin. Following a passage in which Saint Paul speaks about the newness of life of Baptism (Romans 6:1–4), he articulates his ongoing struggle with sin: "For I do not do the good I want, but the evil I do not want is what I do" (Romans 7:19). We share the same struggle. Confession helps us think more clearly about our sins, recognize our need for God's grace to live in a way that pleases him and strengthen our resolve to resist the temptation to sin.

I also need to bless my family by going to Confession regularly. After seeing a particular priest in spiritual direction for a year, I verbalized my discouragement: "Father, I could photocopy my list! I feel like I am saying the same sins every week. Do you see *any* progress?"

He nodded. "Even if all you are doing is humbling yourself to confess the same sins each week, you are taking a whack at pride. And *whatever* takes a whack at pride is a movement in the right direction." (That has become a saying in our family.)

Humility moves us in the right direction. Like the psalmist we pray, "Create in me a clean heart, O God, / and put a new and right spirit within me" (Psalm 51:10). We want to keep moving in the right direction with greater order in our homes, through a plan for cleaning and organization, and greater order in our souls through Confession, by which Jesus unclutters our hearts of sin to make a beautiful home for himself.

PART FIVE

*She
considers
a field
and
buys it*

CHAPTER THIRTEEN

Good Management
in the Garden of the Lord

In imitation of God, men and women enable the land to give glory to God through their stewardship of it. Proverbs 31:16 says, "She considers a field and buys it; / with the fruit of her hands she plants a vineyard." Let's study how to nurture life in the soil and examine parallels with nurturing lives through the sacraments of Matrimony and Holy Orders.

When God created Adam and Eve, he "planted" them in a garden. He gave them several commands as custodians of creation: "And God blessed them, and God said to them, 'Be fruitful and multiply, and fill the earth and subdue it; and have dominion over the fish of the sea and over the birds of the air and over every living thing that moves upon the earth'" (Genesis 1:28).

These commands remain, although Adam and Eve sinned; however, each command has become more difficult due to the consequences of sin. For example, subduing the earth is still necessary, though thorns (or weeds) complicate the task. Our constant struggle against weeds in subduing the earth reflects our own constant struggle with concupiscence— our tendency to sin.

As I was gardening with my son Joseph, who was five at the time, he declared, "Mom, I want to make a time travel machine!"

It seemed like a random thought, and yet he sounded urgent. "Where would you go?" I asked.

"I've *got* to get back to the Garden of Eden. I've got to get to Adam before he sins and tell him, 'Don't do it. It isn't worth it!'"

How true that is! Yet Joseph had no idea that weeds were among the least of the consequences of the Fall with which he would have to contend.

LAND IS A GIFT

When the ark landed safely on Mount Ararat and Noah and his family were able to disembark, the first thing they did was to offer a sacrifice of thanksgiving. The next thing Noah did was to *plant*. "Noah was the first tiller of the soil. He planted a vineyard" (Genesis 9:20).

When God established a covenant with Abraham, he called him from his homeland to give him a promised gift of land, later referred to as "the Promised Land."

> Go from your country and your kindred and your father's house to the land that I will show you. And I will make of you a great nation, and I will bless you, and make your name great, so that you will be a blessing. I will bless those who bless you, and him who curses you, I will curse; and by you all the families of the earth shall bless themselves. (Genesis 12:1–3)

The three blessings of the covenant are land, descendants ("great nation") and a good reputation ("make your name great"). This is *real* wealth.

As a culture, Americans tend to think of money as wealth, but money by itself is sterile; dollars do not produce more dollars. (Some people charge interest; however, the Bible raises many questions about the validity of usury.) In addition, to make more money simply by printing more devalues the dollars already printed, creating inflation. As the saying goes, measure wealth not by the things you have but by the things you have for which you would not take money.

After the Exodus out of Egypt, Moses told the people that God was bringing them to a land flowing with milk and honey, the land of their forefather Abraham. When they arrived at the edge of the Promised Land, Moses sent twelve spies, one from each tribe, to scope out the land and return with eyewitness reports. What they saw was amazing—the land was lush. It took two men to carry one bunch of grapes on a pole between them. However, ten of the spies reported that the people of the land were giants who could not be defeated.

Two faithful spies, Joshua and Caleb, urged the people to trust God's word and to enter the land to conquer it. When the people chose to follow the naysayers rather than trust God, Moses informed them of serious consequences: They would wander in the wilderness for forty years until all adults, except Joshua and Caleb, had died. Since they did not want to go in and possess the land, they would not.

After the forty years passed, Moses led the people of Israel to the edge of the Promised Land again. He knew he would die soon, so he prepared the people of Israel, admonishing them to understand the covenant to which they were committed. These words, as his last teachings to his people, were of paramount importance:

> And all these blessings shall come upon you and overtake
> you, if you obey the voice of the LORD your God. Blessed
> shall you be in the city, and blessed shall you be in the field.
> Blessed shall be the fruit of your body, and the fruit of your
> ground, and the fruit of your beasts, the increase of your
> cattle, and the young of your flock. (Deuteronomy 28:2–4)

Moses linked obedience to God with fruitfulness for them,
their land and their animals.

Then Moses warned them of the consequences of dis-
obeying the covenant:

> But if you will not obey the voice of the LORD your God or
> be careful to do all his commandments and his statutes
> which I command you this day, then all these curses shall
> come upon you and overtake you. Cursed shall you be in
> the city, and cursed shall you be in the field.... Cursed shall
> be the fruit of your body, and the fruit of your ground, the
> increase of your cattle, and the young of your flock.
> (Deuteronomy 28:15–16, 18)

He also linked disobedience to the covenant with barrenness
for them, their land and their animals.

There is an important correlation between obedience and
fruitfulness as a culture on the one hand and disobedience
and a lack of fruitfulness on the other. In Deuteronomy 28
Moses was not addressing individual sins but rather a culture
of sin. When we consider the number of years we have had
legalized abortion in the United States, with the slaughter of
tens of millions of unborn babies, we know that our land has
been polluted with innocent blood. This blood cries out to
God for justice. In addition, the devaluing of human life
through abortion under the guise of a new quality of life ethic

has opened the door to infanticide and euthanasia. As a society, we cannot escape the consequences of such serious sin.

DRY, DESERT LAND

Joshua, as the heir apparent to Moses, led the Israelites into the Promised Land. They entered the gardenlike land out of the desert in which they had been wandering for forty years. Then Joshua conducted a covenant renewal ceremony, warning them that if they should become unfaithful, the Lord would turn this fertile land into a wasteland.

Centuries later, in the late 1800s, Mark Twain visited the Holy Land. He described it as a place of utter desolation. What had once been a land filled with trees and vegetation was now a parched, bleak land.

In the 1990s Scott and I led a couple of tours in Israel. One of our guides commented that the only trees left in Jerusalem from the time of Christ were the olive trees in the Garden of Gethsemane. How could this Promised Land that was once so verdant become so arid? One aspect of the curse for unfaithfulness to the covenant was that the land would become treeless. When this land became treeless, it became a desert.

As we drove through the Judean Desert going toward Jerusalem, we saw mile after mile of the wilderness where Jesus had gone during the days of temptation after his Baptism. This was the same place where hermits in the third, fourth and fifth centuries carved a monastery into a barren hillside. While the tour guide droned on about the innovative solar power that Israel was harnessing in the desert, I thought, *we are missing a great opportunity to teach about the wilderness.* So I walked up the aisle of the bus and requested the microphone.

I asked the people to look around and see the barrenness of the seemingly endless rocks and sand. Nothing was growing. I observed, "This is the state of our souls apart from Christ. But Christ is planting his life deep within us, so that we will produce much fruit. That is how he transforms the desert of our soul into a garden that not only refreshes us but enables us to refresh others."

The prophet Isaiah proclaimed:

When the poor and needy seek water,
    and there is none,
…
I will make the wilderness a pool of water,
    and the dry land springs of water.
…
I will set in the desert the cypress,
    the plane and the pine together;
that men may see and know,
    may consider and understand together,
that the hand of the LORD has done this,
    the Holy One of Israel has created it. (Isaiah 41:17–20)

This is a poignant image: God creates gardens. And where sins make a wilderness, provided there is humility and repentance, God can renew the earth and re-create a well-watered land.

EXPANDING A BOUNDARY

The Proverbs 31 woman is prudent with her family's resources. She is not someone who makes hasty decisions. She looks carefully, so that she can make a wise rather than whimsical purchase. She wants land that is going to be fertile; it needs to have good soil. She is aware that this will be an investment of her time and talent as well as money. So she weighs her decision: Is the property worth the expense? Once the money is spent, it is gone. She knows it is important not to neglect other things by acquiring this one.

In the midst of the genealogy of Judah (which is Jesus' lineage), a righteous prayer of one of his descendants, Jabez, is recorded: "'Oh that you would bless me and enlarge my border, and that your hand might be with me, and that you would keep me from harm so that it might not hurt me!' And God granted what he asked" (1 Chronicles 4:10).

When Jabez prayed for his territory to be enlarged, he anticipated future possibilities. Do we even ask the Lord for this? The purpose of this prayer is not to amass wealth but to have greater stewardship for the honor and glory of God.

Both the desire for an increase of land and the prayer for an increase in the kingdom of God are examples of subduing the earth and having dominion over it, physically and spiritually. We do not need a lot of land to be able to accomplish both, nor should we fear an increase, should God place that in our care.

UNIFIED DREAMS

The Proverbs 31 woman not only considers the possibility of acquiring land but also purchases it. She is an industrious woman. She is not simply consuming the capital of her family; rather, she is finding an effective investment so that the family's earnings multiply under her care.

Recently, in a marriage preparation class, couples were instructed to maintain separate bank accounts after marrying. What a tragedy—to encourage couples entering into a marital union to distrust each other, one pitted against the other financially. The instructor failed to recognize an important teaching related to healthy interdependence: When they marry, they hold all things in common, including their earnings.

The Proverbs 31 woman is not buying and selling property for a job, though there is nothing wrong with being a real estate broker. She is acquiring land to make it productive for the good of her family. Part of good home management involves cultivating a good business sense.

Preparing for the Future

A wise wife finds ways to expand her family's estate. She sets realistic long-term goals with her husband on financial matters. Together they decide what needs to happen to accomplish the goals. The couple can accomplish so much more when they do not allow money concerns to become a tug-of-war between them; rather they choose to pull together as a team.

Financial expert Dave Ramsey explains how a couple's teamwork for financial freedom together is possible. His program is entitled *The Total Money Makeover: A Proven Plan for Financial Fitness*. He shares practical wisdom that is a financial lifeline at a time when a number of young adults are already drowning in debt, feeling trapped by creditors who threaten negative credit reports that could damage their future dreams.[1]

Our culture is a consumer-oriented one, with temptations to spend what we earn, to go into debt through credit cards to get what we want now, so that we are actually spending more than we are earning. Companies even encourage people to borrow on the next paycheck, endangering their ability to pay regular bills while increasing their debt with high interest rates.

As Christians, our goal is not having wealth for its own sake—there are plenty of warnings in Scripture about rich people and the kingdom. Instead our goal is to have resources at our disposal so that we can take advantage of opportunities for stewardship. Poor financial decisions mortgage the future, limiting our choices both for investment and for contributing to the kingdom of God. Good financial decisions help us provide for our families and build the kingdom of God. That takes planning.

PLANTING A VINEYARD

"Every one to whom much is given, of him will much be required" (Luke 12:48b). The godly woman's first step is acquiring the field. The next step she takes is discerning how her land can give glory to God. She can cultivate it either to be beautiful or to produce fruit.

The Proverbs 31 woman plants a vineyard "with the fruit of her hands." It is possible that she uses earnings acquired through her home business (more on that at a later time) and invests them in this field. A more likely interpretation is that she is planting the vineyard with the fruit of her body, meaning her own children assist her. Either way, gardening provides her with an indispensable opportunity to teach her children as they work together.

Her service to her family enables her to subdue the earth while she tills her garden or vineyard. She is personally involved in the cultivation of the vineyard. She does not just send out workers; rather she has dirt under her fingernails as well. She knows there are no quick results; she has to be patient. Pruning and cultivation are required for fruitful resources to become even more fruitful under her care.

Our first landlady in Massachusetts, Lisa, from Scandinavia, loved to work in her garden. One day she declared that the sanest people in the world were farmers and fishermen. She believed they did not lose touch with reality because they never lost touch with the stuff of creation. Farmers and fishermen also seem to have a natural humility— unlike so many people, they do not suffer under the illusion that they are in control of their situation.

LESSONS FROM PLANTING

Rabbis taught a variety of applications from this verse: "You shall keep my statutes. You shall not let your cattle breed with a different kind; you shall not sow your field with two kinds of seed; nor shall there come upon you a garment of cloth made of two kinds of stuff" (Leviticus 19:19).

They applied this teaching of not mixing seeds in a row in a practical way (it is easier to keep track of what seeds or weeds are growing) and also in a spiritual way (as a caution not to be double-minded). Some rabbis also used this verse to caution against believers mixing with nonbelievers: If seeds of deep friendship flower in romance, the couple could experience the difficulties of an ill-advised mixed marriage.

Another passage in the same chapter of Leviticus describes the development of an orchard (see Leviticus 19:23–25). God's people are encouraged to plant fruit trees when they acquire land. However, they should follow a pattern, for practical as well as spiritual reasons, in honoring the Lord.

The first three years' fruit is considered "uncircumcised"; the people are not to pick it. The fourth year's harvest is to be consecrated to the Lord; it should be collected for the priest only. The family demonstrates their trust in the Lord for future harvests by relinquishing this entire first edible crop. The fifth year and all future years, the family is free to harvest for themselves, provided they offer the Lord the first fruits of each harvest and tithe on whatever remains. (Perhaps those of us who garden should also tithe our produce and offer it to a priest or to the poor.)

Another prescription in Leviticus addresses care of the land in giving it a rest from planting every seventh year:

> Say to the sons of Israel, When you come into the land which I give you, the land shall keep a sabbath to the LORD. Six years you shall sow your field, and six years you shall prune your vineyard, and gather in its fruits; but in the seventh year there shall be a sabbath of solemn rest for the land, a sabbath to the LORD; you shall not sow your field or prune your vineyard. (Leviticus 25:2–4)

Even the land needs a sabbath rest. This can be accomplished in different ways. A couple in central Pennsylvania have a large garden in their yard, which they plant for six years and then let lie fallow for the seventh. Many farmers in Africa divide the land into sevenths and let one-seventh rest yearly. This helps the land to be enriched with nutrients so that it yields better harvests in other years.

Soften Fallow Soil

Throughout the Old Testament, when his people's hearts were far from him, the Lord honored the covenant by reducing fruitful places to desolation. When his people repented, the Lord turned the desolate places into fruitful ones. The prophet Hosea warned the people of Israel:

> Sow for yourselves righteousness,
>> reap the fruit of mercy;
>> break up your fallow ground,
> for it is the time to seek the LORD,
>> that he may come and rain salvation upon you.
>> (Hosea 10:12)

Fallow ground is hard-packed soil, unable to receive seeds or properly utilize light and water. It has to be broken and tilled to become usable again. Likewise, God's people have to have the fallow ground of their hardened hearts softened through repentance. If they turn back to him in repentance and belief, seeds of faith sewn in an obedient heart will produce a bountiful harvest of peace and righteousness. It is never too late.

BEING FIRMLY ROOTED

The psalmist contrasts righteous people and wicked people by comparing them to different kinds of vegetation:

> Blessed is the man
>> who walks not in the counsel of the wicked,
> nor stands in the way of sinners,
>> nor sits in the seat of scoffers;
> but his delight is in the law of the LORD,
>> and on his law he meditates day and night.
> He is like a tree
>> planted by streams of water,
> that yields its fruit in its season,
>> and its leaves do not wither.

In all that he does he prospers.
The wicked are not so,
> but are like chaff which the wind drives away.
> (Psalm 1:1–4)

The psalmist paints two vivid pictures: a mammoth tree with deep roots in the earth, which receives water constantly from the flowing stream alongside it; and wind-driven chaff, which is the refuse of good wheat—when the wheat is thrown into the air (which is still done in some third-world countries), the good seed falls to the ground and the worthless chaff blows away. We want to be like the fruitful trees planted by streams of water. And the key to having deep roots, according to the psalmist, is delighting in God's Word, reading it and meditating on it.

Solomon depicts another contrast between the industrious people who keep orderly vineyards versus people whose vineyards reveal their foolishness:

I passed by the field of a sluggard
…
…all overgrown with thorns;
> the ground was covered with nettles,
> and its stone wall was broken down.
> …
> I looked and received instruction.
A little sleep, a little slumber,
> a little folding of the hands to rest,
and poverty will come upon you like a robber,
> and want like an armed man. (Proverbs 24:30–34)

This is the damage that sloth causes.

Frequently the prophets describe God's people as a vineyard. And woe if the Lord finds weeds in his vineyard:

> For the vineyard of the LORD of hosts
>> is the house of Israel,
> and the men of Judah
>> are his pleasant planting;
> and he looked for justice,
>> but behold, bloodshed;
> for righteousness,
>> but behold, a cry!
>> …
>
> The LORD of hosts has sworn in my hearing:
> "Surely many houses shall be desolate,
>> large and beautiful houses, without inhabitant."
>> (Isaiah 5:7, 9)

There are serious consequences when unrighteousness is sown rather than righteousness. However, the Lord is the keeper of his vineyard, and he will do the pruning and tilling that is necessary to restore the vineyard to fruitfulness:

> In that day:
> "A pleasant vineyard, sing of it!
>> I, the LORD, am its keeper;
>> every moment I water it.
> Lest any one harm it,
>> I guard it night and day;
>> …
>
> In days to come Jacob shall take root,
>> Israel shall blossom and put forth shoots,
>> and fill the whole world with fruit." (Isaiah 27:2–3, 6)

Not only does the Lord do this in Isaiah's time, but Isaiah's prophecies apply to the work of the future Messiah.

Judgment will come:

> For the LORD has a day of vengeance,
>   a year of recompense for the cause of Zion.
> …
>
> Thorns shall grow over its strongholds,
>   nettles and thistles in its fortresses. (Isaiah 34:8, 13)

Yet, when the Spirit has gathered God's people as his own possession, "the wilderness and the dry land shall be glad, / the desert shall rejoice and blossom;… For waters shall break forth in the wilderness, / and streams in the desert" (Isaiah 35:1, 6).

The Messiah will restore his people, "for I will pour water on the thirsty land, / and streams on the dry ground; / I will pour my Spirit upon your descendants, / and my blessing on your offspring" (Isaiah 44:3). Not only will the Lord water the dry land, but he will also pour out his Spirit on the land's inhabitants.

We long for the Spirit to be poured out on us and our children, to sow good seed in all of our hearts. It is the Spirit who enables us to share in the Father's love, being rooted in the Son:

> Shower, O heavens, from above,
>   and let the skies rain down righteousness;
> let the earth open, that salvation may sprout forth,
>   and let it cause righteousness to spring up also;
>   I the LORD have created it. (Isaiah 45:8).

Righteousness rains down; righteousness wells up like a spring in a desert.

Rain from heaven, which causes seed to sprout, parallels God's Word, which accomplishes its work in us:

> For as the rain and the snow come down from heaven,
>> and do not return there but water the earth,
> making it bring forth and sprout,
> ...
> so shall my word be that goes forth from my mouth;
>> it shall not return to me empty,
> but it shall accomplish that which I intend,
>> and prosper in the thing for which I sent it. (Isaiah 55:10 11)

God's Word produces fruit. Are we receptive? Do we cultivate it? Isaiah prophesies about the Spirit's work in God's people through the Messiah:

> The Spirit of the Lord GOD is upon me,
>> because the LORD has anointed me
> to bring good tidings to the afflicted;
>> he has sent me to bind up the brokenhearted,
> to proclaim liberty to the captives,
>> and the opening of the prison to those who are bound;
> to proclaim the year of the LORD'S favor,
>> and the day of vengeance of our God;
> ...
> that they may be called oaks of righteousness,
>> the planting of the LORD, that he may be glorified.
>> (Isaiah 61:1–3)

Jesus read this passage from the scroll when he visited his home synagogue in Nazareth. Then he declared that the Scripture had been fulfilled in their hearing (see Luke 4:16–21).

Like the prophets, Jesus referred to gardening in his teachings on the spiritual life. The next chapter examines some of those examples.

CHAPTER FOURTEEN

Cultivating Contemplation

teach children

I can picture the Proverbs 31 woman walking through the field with her children, seizing a teachable moment. "We are going to gather withered branches for the fire tonight. See how this branch's connection to the vine weakened and now it's dead? We have to cut it off and burn it. Don't be like that branch!" Then, coming to a branch laden with fruit, she exclaims, "Ah, see how well connected that branch is to the vine? It already has a cluster of grapes growing. That's the kind of child I want you to be, bearing much fruit!"

Jesus uses a sustained metaphor about a vineyard in describing his disciples' relationship to him and to his Father. "I am the true vine, and my Father is the vinedresser. Every branch of mine that bears no fruit, he takes away" (John 15:1–2).

The vinedresser removes those branches that no longer draw life from the vine. He prunes all extraneous growth, including dead branches that limit fruitfulness. Likewise, the Father prunes us to make us even more fruitful in our spiritual lives.

In 2005 we moved into a new home, which included a well-established vineyard on a hillside. Our first spring there, we attempted to prune the vineyard. That summer the vineyard yielded enough grapes for about two meals. The following spring we pruned it well, following the directions we were given to cut back at least 90 percent of the growth. We were

156

not even sure the vines would survive, but the directions had warned us it would look dead and not to panic. The resultant crop was more than seventy quarts of crushed grapes, canned or frozen, plus fresh grapes for many meals and snacks.

A vinedresser sacrifices the growth of numerous branches and leaves for enriched growth of selected branches, to yield an abundant harvest. In our lives those sacrifices often involve suffering: short-term losses for long-term gains. Suffering is a part of the human condition. If we are not suffering now, it is a lull. The question is whether or not the suffering we experience is an instrument of pruning, so that the Lord of the vineyard will produce the fruit of righteousness in us. Though we may not want to suffer, we do want an abundant harvest of righteousness in our lives.

Sometimes we do not notice how much we rely on our natural virtue and talents to do things for God. However, if we are not abiding in Christ, our efforts fall flat. Jesus cautions his disciples: "You are already made clean by the word which I have spoken to you. Abide in me, and I in you. As the branch cannot bear fruit by itself, unless it abides in the vine, neither can you, unless you abide in me" (John 15:3–4).

We want to bear good fruit, so we must make a home inside ourselves for the Lord and his Word. Saint Paul says, "Let the word of Christ dwell in you richly" (Colossians 3:16). God's Word abides in us through our receiving the Eucharist *and* receiving the written Word of God—knowing it, reading it, memorizing it and meditating on it, as the psalmist says, day and night.

In other words, as Jesus' disciples, we are living branches, thriving as long as we remain connected to Jesus, the vine. It is possible to remain attached, having his life flow through ours; and it is possible to be cut off due to our sin. We do not need to live in fear of being cut off, but we need to cling to Jesus, the one who sustains us.

When we are connected to Christ, his strength flows through us so that we are channels of grace to others. When we sin, we weaken that connection; our sin slows (venial sins) or even blocks (mortal sins) the sap of the life of Christ from coursing through us. We receive the same warning that Jesus gave his disciples:

> I am the vine, you are the branches. He who abides in me, and I in him, he it is that bears much fruit, for apart from me you can do nothing. If a man does not abide in me, he is cast forth as a branch and withers; and the branches are gathered, thrown into the fire and burned. (John 15:5–6)

Apart from Christ we can do nothing of lasting value—in our lives, our marriages or our children's lives. With Christ everything we do has lasting value because of his grace, his divine life at work in and through us. When his Word abides in us, we also receive life because his words are spirit and life:

> As the Father has loved me, so have I loved you; abide in my love. If you keep my commandments, you will abide in my love, just as I have kept my Father's commandments and abide in his love. These things I have spoken to you, that my joy may be in you, and that your joy may be full. (John 15:9 11)

Amid the suffering of pruning, joy is possible. Fullness of joy is what Jesus desires for us. Joy comes from abiding in, resting in and living in obedience to his will.

PARALLELS BETWEEN FAITH AND FARMING

Jesus tells what is now the famous parable of the sower, recorded in Matthew 13:3–9. His focus is less on the sower than on the condition of the soil on receiving the sower's seed. Though Jesus is speaking to a farming community, his listeners do not understand his deeper meaning, so he gives his disciples insights they need to interpret the story properly. His explanation, found in Matthew 13:18–32, could be titled "How is the soil of your soul?"

Seed Sown Along the Path

Jesus explains to his disciples, "Hear then the parable of the sower. When any one hears the word of the kingdom and does not understand it, the Evil One comes and snatches away what is sown in his heart; this is what was sown along the path" (Matthew 13:18–19). *hard-ness of heart*

The earth on a well-worn path is packed down from foot traffic. There is nowhere for the seed to become established. Seed sown along the path lies there, exposed for a bird to seize. The ground has to be broken up in order for seeds to become plants.

If someone hears God's Word with a hardened heart, he or she cannot understand it. We need the Lord to soften any hardness of heart we have, so that the soil of our soul will be prepared for God's Word to take root. When we approach Mass, we do not enter to critique the choir, to scrutinize the job of the altar servers or to analyze the homily. Rather we ask the Lord, what do you want to teach me today? We come with an expectation that the Lord has a word for us—his Spirit wants to speak to our spirit.

I have met many fallen-away Catholics who say they went to Mass and never heard the Gospel. I hear the Gospel at every Mass. I do not know how they missed it, but I do know that the Evil One snatches the seed of the Word before it can produce fruit. When people seem bored at Mass, pray that the Lord will protect them from Satan's attempt to snatch away the seed of God's Word before it can bear fruit in their lives.

Seed Sown on Rocky Ground

Next Jesus describes someone's soul as a mix of dirt and rocks: "This is he who hears the word and immediately receives it with joy; yet he has no root in himself, but endures for a while, and when tribulation or persecution arises on account of the word, immediately he falls away" (Matthew 13:20–21).

This is someone who may have an inspirational experience, such as hearing a moving talk in person or on CD or TV, reading a book, attending a retreat or having a special prayer time. The person's initial response is enthusiastic but not sustainable.

Suffering can uproot fresh spiritual growth. When challenges come, will this person understand the reasons for faith? Like the psalmist, can he acknowledge difficulties and cry to the Lord for help? Nearly a third of the psalms are psalms of complaint, crying out to God for help. Even such complaints are expressions that God can be trusted to help.

In the scorching heat of trials, tribulations and persecutions, if our roots are shallow, our new spiritual growth will wither and die. We may wonder whether or not our faith was ever genuine. We need to remember that our trust in God has to be based on the facts of salvation rather than the feelings from a spiritual experience. Our feelings provide a wonderful consolation of faith, but they are not necessary in order for us to live our lives based on the truths of the faith. We will experience dry or desert times spiritually; we may even suffer what mystics call the "dark night of the soul."

In *Come Be My Light,* Mother Teresa of Calcutta's letters reveal her struggle for more than fifty years. Her feelings of abandonment were real, but she placed her faith in what she knew to be true about God and the mission he had given her. She persevered in faith, and the Lord brought abundant fruit from her life and apostolate.

We need to deepen our growth in the Lord so that when these challenges come—and they will come—we will not be easily uprooted or wither.

Seed Sown Among Thorns

Then Jesus turns the attention of the disciples from the discussion about soil to weeds that grow alongside good plants and destroy the life of good vegetation. "As for what was sown among thorns, this is he who hears the word, but the cares of the world and the delight in riches choke the word, and it proves unfruitful" (Matthew 13:22).

In a garden, for good things to grow, the weeds have to be removed systematically and continually. All gardens have weeds, but the weeds cannot be permitted to choke the life out of the garden.

If we try to add spiritual growth to our lives without dealing with our carnal desires, we discover there is not room for both; Jesus said we cannot serve both God and money (see Matthew 6:24). If we are not diligent, we will allow the cares of this world and a desire for wealth to choke the life of faith in our souls.

My favorite line from the musical *Hello, Dolly!* is spoken by Dolly Levi, quoting her late husband: "Money, pardon the expression, is like manure. It's not worth a thing unless it's spread around, encouraging young things to grow!"[1] If we act as if money is manure, we do not want to hold it for long.

Likewise, we need to exercise stewardship over our money and resources for the kingdom of God, rather than being controlled by a love of money. As we tithe and give alms, we have opportunities to meet the needs around us with what the Lord has placed at our disposal. We acquire possessions and then practice detachment as good stewards. We hear God's Word calling us to care for the poor, the orphans and the widows. We experience a new freedom from the love of money by caring for the needs of others out of our love for God.

Temptations will come to want things and use people. Bills can pile up, so that we question honoring God with tithing. Financial stress can take its toll, especially if we compare our situation to others'. For these weeds to prosper all we have to do is ignore them and they will grow. Instead we need to identify these temptations at an early stage so that, by God's grace, they can be removed. Then spiritual growth can be established.

Flowers and weeds can look similar at first; some weeds can be very attractive. A good spiritual director helps us discern how to detach from the love of money all the while we care for the legitimate needs of our family. And like a garden, the price for fruitfulness will be constant vigilance.

Seed Sown on Good Soil

Jesus' final application of the garden metaphor describes the effect of seed sown where it can truly bear fruit. "As for what was sown on good soil, this is he who hears the word and understands it; he indeed bears fruit, and yields, in one case a hundredfold, in another sixty, and in another thirty" (Matthew 13:23).

We will not all produce the same kind of fruit or the same amount, but we will produce fruit if God's Word takes deep root in our hearts. We want to resist the comparison game, because we are all as different as the flowers of the field. God will produce this good fruit in and through us, provided we have cultivated a soul ready to respond in obedience.

We pray for hearts eager to receive the Word and obey in ways maybe we have not been open to beforehand. We renew our minds, and then we live these truths, loving God more deeply than before by rejecting sin and embracing obedience. We nurture new spiritual growth, taking small steps to bring the lordship of Jesus to bear in each sphere of our lives. The roots have to grow deeply in the garden of our soul before we see the results. We ask the Lord to continue to break up the fallow ground, to water us with the Spirit and to take the time he needs to work in our lives. Good fruit will come if we are rooted in Christ.

Jesus challenged the disciples to discern good from bad teaching:

> Beware of false prophets, who come to you in sheep's clothing but inwardly are ravenous wolves. You will know them by their fruits. Are grapes gathered from thorns, or figs from thistles? So, every sound tree bears good fruit, but the bad tree bears evil fruit. A sound tree cannot bear evil fruit, nor can a bad tree bear good fruit. Every tree that does not bear good fruit is cut down and thrown into

the fire. Thus you will know them by their fruits. (Matthew 7:15–20)

The fruit demonstrates the roots, whether the teaching is from good seeds or weeds. The health of the fruit reveals the health of the tree. May the Lord give us discerning hearts.

PRACTICAL LIFE LESSONS FROM THE GARDEN

Saint Paul praises the Corinthians for their generous spirit:

> The point is this: he who sows sparingly will also reap sparingly, and he who sows bountifully will also reap bountifully. Each one must do as he has made up his mind, not reluctantly or under compulsion, for God loves a cheerful giver.... He who supplies seed to the sower and bread for food will supply and multiply your resources and increase the harvest of your righteousness. (2 Corinthians 9:6–7, 10)

A lesson from the garden shows us that the harvest reflects how generously the seed was sown. Likewise, there is a direct connection between how generous we are with the Lord and the harvest of righteousness that he produces in and through us. We cannot take shortcuts in holy living and think we will have an abundance of happiness and holiness in our families. Both in our attitudes (giving cheerfully) and in our actions (giving abundantly) we trust the Lord to increase our faith.

To the Galatians Saint Paul teaches a different principle from the garden: "Do not be deceived; God is not mocked, for whatever a man sows, that he will also reap. For he who sows to his own flesh will from the flesh reap corruption; but he who sows to the Spirit will from the Spirit reap eternal life" (Galatians 6:7–8).

Farmers know this well: If you sow beans, you harvest beans; if you sow corn, you harvest corn. Obviously. We reap what we sow—in the flesh or in the Spirit. If we sow wild oats in sin, we will reap corruption; if we sow in the Spirit, we will reap eternal life. Sometimes we deceive ourselves into thinking that how we live does not have eternal consequences, but it does.

Farming is difficult but necessary work, requiring strength and stamina. Farmers face challenges with the elements that they cannot control and related financial risks. Many of us in other careers retain an illusion of control; farmers do not. Farmers have a natural dependence on God, a respect for what they can do and what only God can do. "Do not hate toilsome labor, / or farm work, which were created by the Most High" (Sirach 7:15).

Perhaps this is one of the reasons why monasteries always seem to develop gardens or subsistence farming. Their cultivation of natural life provides a backdrop for their cultivation of the contemplative life. Apart from the financial benefit to the monastery—saving money on groceries—there is the satisfaction that comes from consuming what you have produced. "You shall eat the fruit of the labor of your hands; / you shall be happy, and it shall be well with you" (Psalm 128:2).

When we cultivate gardens, we nurture life. "Human beings were made to interact with growing things."[2] It is good for our health. In addition, beauty makes us long for God, especially in nature. Allowing beauty into our lives is not contrary to the will to sacrifice, either in the monastery or in our homes.

HOW TO TEND A GARDEN

Whether we place plants in pots or farm plots, plant shrubbery for hedges or vines, train vegetation to climb a trellis or an arbor or try container gardening, we need to follow certain steps to nurture growth.

We select the area to garden, making sure it can receive adequate light and water for our plants to thrive. Next we prepare the soil, carefully removing rocks and breaking up fallow ground. We replenish the soil with nutrients through mulched matter, and we remove any weeds that have already begun to grow.

Any package of seeds will give us the essential information of how to plant: the optimal growing season for a given area, what depth and how close together to plant the seeds. It is easier for us to distinguish weeds from fledgling plants if we limit a row to one kind of seed.

Companion gardens are a mix of vegetables or herbs with flowers. They form a symbiotic relationship that contributes to pest control by repelling some insects and encouraging others that are helpful. This results in better yields of vegetables or herbs and larger flowers. For more information about companion gardens and combinations that work best in your area, see the Gardens Ablaze Web site.[3]

Currently there is a revival of Mary Gardens in the United States. During medieval times gardeners renamed hundreds of flowers "as symbols of the life, mysteries and privileges of the Blessed Virgin Mary, Mother of Jesus."[4] An extensive list is available that compares common flower names and names related to Mary.[5]

Raised beds can be a helpful way to plant on a hillside. Create boxes with one-by-six-inch pine boards, joining them with screws at an angle. (Do not use pressure-treated lumber, since you do not want the chemicals used on the boards to be absorbed by your produce.) Fill the bottom two inches of the box with soil from the hillside, add two inches of topsoil mixed with compost, and top with an inch of mulch. Since you will walk around the boxes to weed and to harvest, you will not pack down the soil. This enables the water and nutrients to be absorbed more easily by the plants.

Once you have planted the garden, cover the ground around the plants with shredded newspaper (black and white print only) and a layer of mulch (which also keeps the newspaper from blowing away). This helps the ground retain water longer and inhibits weed growth. Once the garden is established, a maintenance schedule is needed for systematic weeding. Weeds tend to grow faster and in more places than good plants, and they can spread. It is important to eradicate the weeds' roots before they multiply.

Gardening requires diligence and patience. Living things grow little by little, and you cannot skip a step just to hurry along the process. You can make the job easier by including others in the project and using work time as an opportunity for conversation. It is amazing what teens will tell you when they are working at your side. And when you share the work, you all enjoy sharing the harvest.

GRANDMA HAHN'S ORCHARD

The day after I taught this material, I glanced out back and realized that we had a patch of land beyond the swing set that had grown up helter-skelter. I needed to help this land give glory to God—now was the time to cultivate it. Besides, my mother-in-law had given us money that we wanted to use for something special. Since there seems to be a Hahn family tradition of planting fruit trees, we decided to plant fruit trees behind the children's play area.

I began clearing the land with my children, not knowing what shape it would take. At first we cut down miscellaneous trees and uprooted thick wild grape vines. Then we planted vines and pachysandra to hold the top of the hillside while we cleared more land. Soon we knew that more than plants would be needed to keep the hillside from sliding, so we terraced the hillside with retaining walls, five on each side, and added steps to make it easier to climb up and down the hill.

We had no idea how prayerful this place could be. As we worked, we were surrounded by many birds and a sense of being in a wood, though we were in town. How could we make prayer an even more intimate part of this place? What came to my heart was placing Stations of the Cross around the perimeter, if we built a six-foot-high fence to enclose it. Gabriel and I built the fence—he drove every screw while I held each board in place.

In 1998, at Pentecost, Scott purchased our Stations of the Cross in Rome and carried the heavy packages to a papal audience, where John Paul II, Servant of God,[6] gave his blessing to religious objects. Months later a dear friend from Ireland designed the containers for each station, modeled after the tabernacle at Franciscan University's *Portiuncula*, and our sons Michael and Gabriel helped him build and mount them.

Since Franciscans are the keepers of the holy places in Israel, they have the right before any bishop to specially bless Stations of the Cross so that an indulgence is attached to praying them in a particular location. On the Feast of Saint Francis, 1999, Father Richard Davis gave this blessing to our Stations. Now someone praying the Stations in our orchard can receive an indulgence, provided other requirements for the indulgence—Confession and Communion—are met within a few days of the prayer.

All of our children and many of our neighbors' children helped us clear the land, establish the vegetation, maintain weed control, carry bricks to pave the paths and walkways and harvest the fruit. Our conversations were memorable in the midst of sweating, bleeding and getting dirt everywhere together. We also had considerable help from the people who lived with us during that time, including Juliette and David, Michael, Chris and Alfredo (who affectionately dubbed our project "the Widowmaker," wondering whether or not they would survive the ordeal).

Little did I know that when we began to clear the hillside, eventually we would have a terraced hillside with twenty fruit trees surrounded by blessed Stations of the Cross enclosed by a six-foot-high fence. What a joy that orchard has become, a place of prayer and peace! It is still a lot of work to maintain, but it yields a lot of different kinds of fruit, not the least of which is contemplative prayer and reflection.

TEND THE LORD'S GARDEN WITHIN

How do we tend the gardens of our souls and the souls in our care?

We ask the Spirit to soften any hardness in our hearts so that we are prepared to hear God's Word and have it take root. We know that sins need to be removed, and the best way to remove them is to get at the root sins. Confession and spiritual direction help us to identify them and work to get rid of them. Then even our sins, through Confession and penance, become a source of grace. This also helps us root out venial sins that could beat down the path to mortal sins, for we know that chaos in our spiritual life will not bear good fruit.

Many lessons we learned as we developed the orchard have made even greater sense in "keeping" the garden of our souls. For years we had dumped leaves and branches in a pile in the orchard. When we turned over the soil, we realized that the compost had become rich, black soil.

"That's Confession!" I exclaimed to one of my children as we worked. "We bring our sins, weaknesses and failures—the refuse of our lives—to the Lord, and he turns them into the mulch of a renewed spiritual life! Our sins have an even greater stench than the garbage composting in our garden, and yet God can use anything given to him. We leave the confessional with grace, with courage, with faith, with a renewed desire to say no to self and yes to God."

Besides good soil, we seek the light of the Word of God to nurture our soul. And we pray for the Spirit to rain down righteousness so that righteousness will grow in our hearts. We allow the Lord to prune as needed through mortification and suffering, especially unjust suffering, so that we will be more fruitful.

All of this requires vigilance and patience. Spiritual growth, like growth in a garden, is slow, almost imperceptible at times, and steady. If we persist in faithfulness, there will be an abundant harvest in our lives, our marriages, our families, the Church, our culture and our world.

CHAPTER FIFTEEN

A Mother's Guide
to the Sacraments of Consecration:
Holy Orders and Holy Matrimony

Through the sacraments of initiation—Baptism, Confirmation and Holy Communion—we become children of God and disciples of Christ. We are consecrated or set apart as "a chosen race, a royal priesthood, a holy nation, God's own people, that you may declare the wonderful deeds of him who called you out of darkness into his marvelous light" (1 Peter 2:9). We participate in Christ's priesthood as we assist in offering the Mass, in Christ's prophetic mission to proclaim salvation to the world and in Christ's kingship as we bring the lordship of Christ to bear in every sphere of our lives.

How do we carry out these roles? Our initial consecration prepares us for a particular consecration in the sacraments of either Holy Orders or Holy Matrimony, however God leads. In a sense, our particular consecration gives us our marching orders, guiding us in how to serve Christ.

The *Catechism* explains the mission of men who are ordained to the ministerial priesthood. "Those who receive the sacrament of Holy Orders are *consecrated* in Christ's name 'to feed the Church by the word and grace of God' " [*LG* 11§2] (*CCC*, 1535). Men and women who receive the sacrament of

Holy Matrimony are also consecrated for a particular mission. "Christian spouses are fortified and, as it were, *consecrated* for the duties and dignity of their state by a special sacrament" [*GS* 48§2] (*CCC,* 1535).

Like the sacraments of initiation, the sacraments of Holy Orders and Holy Matrimony contribute to our salvation, providing a particular path for us to grow in holiness. Even more, they provide "a particular mission in the Church and serve to build up the People of God" (*CCC,* 1534). The call to priesthood is not a general call but rather a particular call to serve a certain diocese or order. The call to marriage is not a general call but rather a call to a specific man or woman. We may have a sense of God's call on our lives, but it has to be confirmed by an actual call.

One day I was quietly gardening alongside my son Jeremiah, who was five years old, when all of a sudden he turned to me and voiced his discouragement.

"I pray and I pray and I pray, and God doesn't answer!"

Surprised at how disheartened he sounded, I inquired, "What are you praying about, Jeremiah?"

"I ask God what is my mission in life, and he won't tell me!"

At the end of Mass, I often prayed with our children that God would reveal to them their mission in life. His prayer had probably echoed my own. What could I offer that would diminish his sense that God was not listening to his earnest question?

"Jer, you know how much you talk about India and your desire for the people of India to be Christians?" For some reason it had been on his heart to ask siblings and visitors if they wanted to go to India to tell people about Jesus. "Maybe your mission in life is to be a priest and go to India to spread the gospel."

"I don't want to be a priest!" he replied quickly.

Wrong track, I thought. "Honey, that's fine. You don't have to be a priest," I reassured him. The last thing I wanted to do was to pressure him about being a priest. "Maybe the Lord has a little girl named Beth who someday you will meet and marry."

"I don't want to be married!" he responded emphatically.

Now I was really confused. "What do you *want* to be, Jer?"

"I just want to be a little boy!"

I smiled. I think God smiled too. "Jeremiah, that *is* your mission for now. And when your mission changes, God will tell you."

He hugged me; he was so relieved. I did not realize that my prayer had overwhelmed him. We can be overwhelmed by God's call on our lives too, especially when it comes to training our children in the spiritual life.

How can we best prepare our children for God's call on their lives? We pray for them and with them, that they will yield their hearts and lives completely to the Lord. We prepare them to be faithful spouses and fruitful parents. We find ways to support them as they venture out to test God's call on their lives. Finally, we seek to live our own vocation in the most beautiful way we can, so that they are strengthened by our Lord's faithful love in us.

Most Catholics are called to be consecrated in marriage. We freely consent to give ourselves as gifts to each other, open to life and the sacrifices of love.

We recognize that our marriage witnesses to the relationship between Christ and the Church, no matter how imperfectly we may live it. Saint Paul says: "'For this reason a man shall leave his father and mother and be joined to his wife, and the two shall become one flesh.' This is a great mystery, and I mean in reference to Christ and the Church" (Ephesians 5:31–32).

Christ and the Church are united in faithful and fruitful love. We reflect this mystery through our committed love, genuine respect and self-donating sacrificial service. Our intimate union, consecrated to the Lord, will bear great fruit spiritually and, by the grace of God, physically as well, building up the Church in a variety of ways.

God has a wonderful plan for your life. If you are married, your spouse is an integral part of that plan. The Lord is the one who has called you to marriage. He is the source of the love that sustains you, the strength that fortifies you and the grace that enables you to sacrifice for each other. He will guide you through the challenges of married life, so that your sacrificial self-giving flows from and deepens faithful and fruitful love. And he will enable you both to assist each other on the path to heaven.

The Lord is cultivating his life in you for the purpose of greater fruitfulness. He wants to uproot all that is not of him in the garden of your soul, so that he can draw you into the closest possible relationship to him. And then he wants to reproduce his fruitfulness through you, extending his life in your family and beyond your family to the world.

PART SIX

*She
girds
herself
with
strength*

CHAPTER SIXTEEN

Gird Your Loins With Strength

One man wrote, "I know I'm not going to understand women. I'll never understand how you can take boiling hot wax, pour it onto your upper thigh, rip the hair out by the root, and still be afraid of a spider."[1] Women have strength of which men know not; we also have weaknesses we struggle to admit.

When we examine the many details of life involved in homemaking, we can become overwhelmed and discouraged or feel defeated—so many tasks to do and so little time in which to do them. And the job is even bigger when we factor in caring for the souls of the precious people under our roof. How can we accomplish such a demanding job?

To do God's work God's way, we prepare ourselves physically and spiritually to meet the challenges in *his* strength. We acknowledge the variety of talents, skills, abilities, energy, experience and knowledge that God has given us. We recognize that God has designed women to desire deeper interpersonal connections, heart to heart, so that through our friendships with other women, we strengthen each other. When we utilize all of these gifts, relying on the power of the Spirit, we honor the Lord.

SHE PREPARES FOR ACTIVE WORK

The Proverbs 31 woman is a woman of strength. "She clothes her loins with strength / and makes her arms strong"

(Proverbs 31:17). She serves God with her whole body, loving him with all her might (see Deuteronomy 6:5; Matthew 22:37–38). From the fullness of strength (from the Lord), she makes her arms firm and strong.

She tucks her free-flowing garment into her sash to prepare for her work, imitating God, who girds up his loins as he establishes creation: "Who by your strength have established the mountains, / being girded with might" (Psalm 65:6). By his strength we also can be creative in our work.

She exercises authority over her land just as the Lord rules over the earth by his sovereignty:

> The LORD reigns; he is robed in majesty;
>> the LORD is robed, he is girded with strength.
> Yes, the world is established; it shall never be moved;
>> your throne is established from of old;
>> you are from everlasting. (Psalm 93:1–2)

We imitate the Lord, girding ourselves with his strength to reign over our realm.

SHE MAKES HER ARMS STRONG

This is not a picture of parlor ladies who look incapable of being intelligent or productive. Nor is this a picture of a manly woman, declaring her ability to do anything a man can do. This is a picture of a woman who uses her whole body to serve the Lord wholeheartedly, for she knows the greatest commandment begins with these words, "Hear, O Israel: The LORD our God is one LORD; and you shall love the LORD your God with all your heart, and with all your soul, and with all your *might*" (Deuteronomy 6:4–5, italics added).

Physical labor is a way to love the Lord. It is not beneath the dignity of a woman of God to work. Rather, it is an expression of her dignity to work and to work diligently.

The woman of God responds to the needs of her family. Whereas a single woman might have a regular exercise regime at the gym, a young mother, who has less time to lift weights, does her weight lifting as she carries her baby, a booster seat or car seat and a diaper bag! As her baby grows, she is amazed at how strong she has made her arms. The strength comes as she responds to her family's needs.

The Lord is the source of strength. When he addresses Cyrus, king of Persia, the Lord reveals himself as the one who empowered Cyrus to conquer Babylon and now calls him to return Israel from exile to the Promised Land.

> For the sake of my servant Jacob,
>   and Israel my chosen,
> I call you by your name,
>   I surname you, though you do not know me.
> I am the LORD, and there is no other,
>   besides me there is no God;
>   I clothe you, though you do not know me,
> that men may know, from the rising of the sun
>   and from the west, that there is none besides me;
>   I am the LORD, and there is no other. (Isaiah 45:4–6)

Whether or not King Cyrus acknowledges it, the Lord is the one who is providing the strength with which he rules.

Our daughters have strength they may not yet realize. King David prayed for God's blessing on the children of Israel, "May our sons in their youth / be like plants full grown, / our daughters like corner pillars / cut for the structure of a palace"

(Psalm 144:12). Initially our daughters may not think it a compliment when we refer to them as pillars, unless they consider what palace pillars were: beautiful and ornate, sculpted works of art, created through careful planning and hard work. They were set on a firm foundation to bear the weight of the palace roof. They were created by people of strength so that they could contribute strength.

In the Old Testament, people girded their loins with strength for one of five primary tasks: for battle, with inner courage to face trials, for priestly duty, to prepare for repentance and to work diligently. They needed God's strength to tackle each task, just as the Proverbs 31 woman girded her loins with the strength of the Lord to fulfill God's call on her life. We will briefly examine each of these tasks and how they apply to us today.

GIRD YOUR LOINS FOR BATTLE

God arms his people with power for battle, so that his enemies will fail. Though women have rarely been at the forefront of actual battles, a few women have played key roles in defeating Israel's enemies. Two examples are Jael and Judith.

When the military leader Barak is summoned before the prophetess Deborah to hear how the Lord will win the battle, Barak doubts God's word and refuses to enter battle unless Deborah accompanies him. Deborah responds, "I will surely go with you; nevertheless, the road on which you are going will not lead to your glory, for the LORD will sell Sisera into the hand of a woman" (Judges 4:9). Though Barak leads the army to route General Sisera's army, Sisera escapes and finds shelter in a woman's—Jael's—tent. Once he falls asleep, she drives a tent peg through his temple.

Another example of a woman who defeats Israel's enemy is Judith. Standing by the bed of Holofernes, leader of the Assyrian army, Judith prays, "O Lord God of all might, look in this hour upon the work of my hands for the exaltation of Jerusalem. For now is the time to help your inheritance, and to carry out my undertaking for the destruction of the enemies who have risen up against us" (Judith 13:4–5). She then takes Holofernes's own sword, holds his head by his hair and says, "Give me strength this day, O Lord God of Israel!" (Judith 13:7). She strikes his neck twice with all her might and cuts off his head.

In Genesis 3:15 God declares enmity between the snake and the woman and between their seeds. This refers to the conflict between the devil and Mary as well as the devil's mortal combat with her "seed," Jesus, who will be victorious. Mary is a picture or type of the Church, so that Saint Paul refers to believers' spiritual conflict with and eventual victory over the Evil One in terms similar to the Genesis 3:15 passage: "For while your obedience is known to all, so that I rejoice over you, I would have you wise as to what is good and guileless as to what is evil; then the God of peace will soon crush Satan under your feet" (Romans 16:19–20).

God's people place their trust in him rather than in horses, warriors or armies. King David proclaims:

> For who is God, but the LORD?
>> And who is a rock, except our God?—
> the God who girded me with strength,
>> and made my way safe.
> …
> For you girded me with strength for the battle;
>> you made my assailants sink under me. (Psalm 18:31–32, 39)

The Lord's strength, rather than the king's army, procures the victory:

> A king is not saved by his great army;
> > a warrior is not delivered by his great strength.
> The war horse is a vain hope for victory,
> > and by its great might it cannot save.
>
> Behold, the eye of the LORD is on those who fear him,
> > on those who hope in his merciful love,
> that he may deliver their soul from death,
> > and keep them alive in famine. (Psalm 33:16–19)

David contrasts the sources of strength in battle that people perceive as the sources of victory (the king, a great army or a war horse) with the true source of strength in the battle, the Lord. David does not mean that anyone should enter battle unarmed. Rather, those in battle need to note their dependence upon the Lord:

> Gird your sword upon your thigh, O mighty one,
> > in your glory and majesty!
>
> In your majesty ride forth victoriously
> > for the cause of truth and to defend the right;
> > let your right hand teach you dread deeds!
> Your arrows are sharp
> > in the heart of the king's enemies;
> > the peoples fall under you. (Psalm 45:3–5)

God's power protects his people, especially through prayer and worship:

> Ascribe power to God,
> > whose majesty is over Israel,
> > and his power is in the skies.

> Awesome is God in his sanctuary,
>> the God of Israel,
>> he gives power and strength to his people.
>
> Blessed be God! (Psalm 68:34–35).

As Americans, we may not need to be ready for a battle in our streets, but we do need to prepare for the spiritual warfare that occurs daily. This is not just for the saints among us—*all* of us are vulnerable. We forget we are in a battle; we forget to put on our armor, as described by Saint Paul:

> Finally, be strong in the Lord and in the strength of his might. Put on the whole armor of God, that you may be able to stand against the wiles of the devil. For we are not contending against flesh and blood, but against the principalities, against the powers, against the world rulers of this present darkness, against the spiritual hosts of wickedness in the heavenly places. Therefore take the whole armor of God, that you may be able to withstand in the evil day, and having done all, to stand. Stand therefore, having fastened the belt of truth around your waist, and having put on the breastplate of righteousness, and having shod your feet with the equipment of the gospel of peace; besides all these, taking the shield of faith, with which you can quench all the flaming darts of the Evil One. And take the helmet of salvation, and the sword of the Spirit, which is the word of God. Pray at all times in the Spirit, with all prayer and supplication. (Ephesians 6:10–18)

There are obvious attacks, and there are subtle challenges in spiritual warfare. How can we prepare?

First, we ensure our defensive armor is in place. The Lord provides by his grace the protection we need to safeguard our hearts, our minds and our souls from the attacks of the Evil One. The Lord is the one who arms us.

Second, we use the offensive weapons of Scripture (the sword of the Spirit) and prayer. We need to learn the Word of God, study it and memorize it so that we can meditate on it and live it well. Our model is Jesus. When Satan attacks him after his Baptism by twisting Scripture out of context to tempt him, Jesus refutes him with Scripture. We need to imitate Jesus by wielding the sword of the Spirit too.

Prayer is our other offensive weapon. Prayer helps us draw on God's strength, so that we do not enter spiritual conflict relying on ourselves. The Evil One wants us to doubt God's presence and to mistrust God's power; prayer affirms both God's presence and power in our lives. Saint John encourages us, "Little children, you are of God, and have overcome them; for he who is in you is greater than he who is in the world" (1 John 4:4). We assault the kingdom of darkness as we intercede for ourselves and others. Prayer is powerful.

We need to remember that the battle is not between my spouse and me or my child and me. The battle is for the formation of our souls in building the kingdom of God. The battle is interior, as we yield more of ourselves to the Lord; and it is exterior, as we expose what is evil and cling to what is good. We pray for heroic virtue to be faithful to the end.

Gird Your Loins
With Inner Courage to Face Trials
The book of Job records the trials that Job faces. For a long time Job does not turn on God. However, he reaches a point when he challenges God. God's response is to challenge Job:

"Gird up your loins like a man, / I will question you, and you shall declare to me" (Job 38:3). In a sense God's challenge is to place Job in the dock, on trial, to face questions. When Job responds with meekness, the Lord rewards his righteousness.

Years later Joshua readies the people to enter the Promised Land, following the death of Moses, the Israelites' beloved leader for forty years. The Lord reminds Joshua, "Have I not commanded you? Be strong and of good courage; be not frightened, neither be dismayed; for the LORD your God is with you wherever you go" (Joshua 1:9). God promises that his strength will sustain Joshua as he leads God's people.

The Proverbs 31 woman girds her loins with strength, for "strength and dignity are her clothing, / and she laughs at the time to come" (Proverbs 31:25). She does not laugh because she is silly but rather because she is confident in the Lord. She does not know the future, but she knows the One who knows the future. This inspires her with courage to face trials and tribulations.

Likewise, Saint Paul assures his disciple Timothy:

God did not give us a spirit of timidity but a spirit of power and love and self-control.

Do not be ashamed then of testifying to our Lord, nor of me his prisoner, but take your share of suffering for the gospel in the power of God. (2 Timothy 1:7–8)

Like Saint Timothy, we have received the Holy Spirit through Baptism and have been sealed in the Spirit through Confirmation. This is the Spirit who releases God's power in our lives so that we can bear testimony faithfully.

Saint Paul challenges Timothy to prepare: "Do your best to present yourself to God as one approved, a workman who has no need to be ashamed, rightly handling the word of truth" (2 Timothy 2:15). Saint Paul has already experienced the power of God, as he bears testimony: "But the Lord stood by me and gave me strength to proclaim the word fully, that all the Gentiles might hear it" (2 Timothy 4:17). Likewise, we can rely on the Lord to give us the right words when we face trials; however, we also need to prepare to give an answer for the hope that we have.

Following the great chapter of the heroes and heroines of the faith—Hebrews 11—the writer challenges us, "Consider him who endured from sinners such hostility against himself, so that you may not grow weary or fainthearted. In your struggle against sin you have not yet resisted to the point of shedding your blood" (Hebrews 12:3–4). By God's strength we can have heroic virtue.

Saint Peter also urges us, "Therefore gird up your minds, be sober, set your hope fully upon the grace that is coming to you at the revelation of Jesus Christ" (1 Peter 1:13). To gird our loins in order to answer a challenge includes girding our minds with truth. We need to know why we believe what we believe. Then we can prepare our children to understand the Faith, so that they can answer the challenges they will inevitably face.

GIRD YOUR LOINS FOR PRIESTLY DUTY

When Moses brought the people of Israel out of Egypt to Mount Sinai, he met with the Lord and received this word for the Israelites:

> You have seen what I did to the Egyptians, and how I bore you on eagles' wings and brought you to myself. Now

> therefore, if you will obey my voice and keep my covenant, you shall be my own possession among all peoples; for all the earth is mine, and you shall be to me a kingdom of priests and a holy nation. These are the words which you shall speak to the children of Israel. (Exodus 19:4–6)

Originally the Israelites were called as a kingdom of priests to bring truth to all nations; in many ways they failed in this mission. As a consequence of their covenant breaking in worshipping the golden calf at Mount Sinai, the priesthood was transferred from the firstborn sons to the Levites (see Numbers 1—6).

God vested his people with strength for priestly duty. Before the Levites were ordained to the priesthood, Aaron and his sons were girded in priestly garb: "You shall gird them with girdles and bind caps on them; and the priesthood shall be theirs by a perpetual statute. Thus you shall ordain Aaron and his sons" (Exodus 29:9, *RSVCE*).

King David understood his call to priestly kingship. For instance, he led the procession of the return of the ark of the covenant to Jerusalem: "And David danced before the LORD with all his might; and David was belted with a linen ephod [priestly garb]. So David and all the house of Israel brought up the ark of the LORD with shouting, and with the sound of the horn" (2 Samuel 6:14–15). David led the procession dressed as a priest, he had musicians play the music he had prepared for the liturgical celebration, and then he offered sacrifices.

The Proverbs 31 woman has a heart for God, and her family knows it. They bless her for her faithfulness, and they praise her for her good works that flow from a life of faith. "Charm is deceitful, and beauty is vain, / but a woman who fears the LORD is to be praised. / Give her of the fruit of her hands, / and let her works praise her in the gates" (Proverbs 31:30–31). Her good works bear testimony to God's work in her life.

In Christ we receive Israel's original call to priesthood and kingship. Saint John writes, "To him who loves us and has freed us from our sins by his blood and made us a kingdom, priests to his God and Father, to him be glory and dominion for ever and ever. Amen" (Revelation 1:5–6). By virtue of our Baptism, we participate in Christ's roles as priest, prophet and king.

We are restored as a kingdom of priests—a different priesthood than the ordained priesthood, with its unique role *in persona Christi,* but a genuine priesthood of all believers through our participation in the offering of the Mass. The bread and wine represent us and our self-offering; the Spirit transforms our gift into the gift of Christ's own body and blood, our Lord's self-offering re-presented. We are not passive observers but active participants in the Eucharistic celebration.

We have a prophetic role. Prophets, like Jeremiah, were commanded, "But you, gird up your loins; arise, and say to them everything that I command you. Do not be dismayed by them, lest I dismay you before them" (Jeremiah 1:17). Likewise, without embarrassment, we are to speak God's Word to one another.

We also have a part in Christ's kingship, bringing his heavenly reign to bear on earth. God empowers all of us to be faithful to our vocations, to live God's calling with his power. If we desire our families to be holy, we need to do it God's way. And yet many times we fail, as did Israel. Then what are we to do?

GIRD YOUR LOINS TO PREPARE FOR REPENTANCE

The prophets warn the people to repent publicly so that they might stave off God's wrath. Jeremiah proclaims God's impending judgment in Jerusalem, telling the people to repent. "For this clothe yourself with sackcloth, / lament and wail; / for the fierce anger of the LORD / has not turned back from us" (Jeremiah 4:8). The prophet Joel also warns of the Day of Judgment:

> Gird on sackcloth and lament, O priests,
>   wail, O ministers of the altar.
> Go in, pass the night in sackcloth,
>   O ministers of my God!
> Because cereal offering and drink offering
>   are withheld from the house of your God.
>
> Sanctify a fast,
>   call a solemn assembly.
> Gather the elders
>   and all the inhabitants of the land
> to the house of the LORD your God;
>   and cry to the LORD. (Joel 1:13–14, *RSVCE*)

True repentance expresses the humility God wants from each of us. Humility is a fruit of the kind of fear of the Lord exemplified by the Proverbs 31 woman. "By loyalty and faithfulness iniquity is atoned for, / and by the fear of the LORD a man [or woman] avoids evil" (Proverbs 16:6).

The women (see 2 Maccabees 3:19) and the men with Maccabeus (see 2 Maccabees 10:25) gird their loins with sackcloth as a sign of repentance and a plea for deliverance from a powerful enemy. The Lord gives them power to overcome so that, with the psalmist, they can say,

> You have turned for me my mourning into dancing;
>> you have loosed my sackcloth
>> and clothed me with gladness,
> that my soul may praise you and not be silent.
>> O LORD my God, I will give thanks to you for ever.
>> (Psalm 30:11–12)

By God's grace we realize our sinfulness and repent. We have to be careful not to presume upon his grace and take our sins lightly. As Saint Paul says, "Or do you presume upon the riches of his kindness and forbearance and patience? Do you not know that God's kindness is meant to lead you to repentance?" (Romans 2:4) Let's gird our loins in repentance so that we can know the joy of our salvation.

GIRD YOUR LOINS TO WORK DILIGENTLY

God equips his people with might, to obey without hesitation. Moses describes how the people are to prepare for and then partake in the Passover: "In this manner you shall eat it: your loins girded, your sandals on your feet, and your staff in your hand; and you shall eat it in haste. It is the LORD'S Passover" (Exodus 12:11). They are to be ready to respond quickly when the Lord delivers them.

Twice the prophet Elisha commands someone to gird his loins and go without delay on an errand for the Lord (see 2 Kings 4:29; 9:1). In both cases the one sent responds immediately and obeys the Word of the Lord.

The Proverbs 31 woman is preparing for her day's labor when she girds her loins, gathering her physical strength to do the task and the spiritual reserves to do it for the Lord. As a faithful servant of the Lord, this model for godly wives and mothers knows the source of her strength.

Jesus advises the disciples to be watchful and faithful as servants of the master:

> Let your loins be girded and your lamps burning, and be like men who are waiting for their master to come home from the marriage feast, so that they may open to him at once when he comes and knocks. Blessed are those servants whom the master finds awake when he comes; truly, I say to you, he will put on his apron and have them sit at table, and he will come and serve them. (Luke 12:35–37)

Jesus demonstrates this teaching in the Upper Room, when he removes his outer garments and girds himself with a towel in order to wash the disciples' feet (see John 13:4–5). Jesus' humble example of service just before his death illustrates the kind of servant leadership that our lives should exemplify, beginning with those closest to us and extending to others.

GOD IS OUR STRENGTH

The Lord helps us to keep the big picture in mind, to discern the eternal meaning behind the challenges, joys and sufferings we experience each day. Like the psalmist, we can say, "Blessed are the men whose strength is in you, / in whose heart are the highways to Zion" (Psalm 84:5).

When we face difficulty, our heavenly Father's strength sustains us, for "God is our refuge and strength, / a very present help in trouble" (Psalm 46:1). The Lord is the one who gives us strength by arming us for spiritual warfare, preparing us for answering objections to the faith, empowering us as a kingdom of priests for faithfulness to our vocations, leading us to repentance and equipping us to grow in diligent service to him.

CHAPTER SEVENTEEN

God's Strength for Us

Current American culture promotes opposing views of women. On the one hand, many people encourage women to utilize their intellects, talents and skills through better education and a career. Opportunities have opened to women that in previous centuries were not possible. On the other hand, many discourage young women from choosing to use those same gifts in service to a husband and children. As women, we can feel torn by others' expectations and our own heart's desires; we have many choices to make and challenges to meet. The critical question is, will we be proud and attempt to resolve these questions on our own? Or will we humble ourselves before God and ask him for strength to meet the difficulties? Drawing closer to him is important. Not only does the Lord have strength, but he *is* strength.

THE STRENGTH OF THE PROUD

If we gird our loins with our own strength, God may be the one who will undo it. "With God are wisdom and might; / he has counsel and understanding. / ... / He pours contempt on princes, / and looses the belt of the strong" (Job 12:13, 21). In essence, God declares, if you try to make yourself strong, I will make you weak, *for your sake.*

Throughout the books of Joshua and Judges, the Israelites are warned against pride. Over and over they repeat a cycle.

First, they do evil, and God gives them over to their enemies. Next, they humble themselves to ask the Lord for help. God hears their cries and sends a deliverer, who conquers their enemies and brings peace. Then the people take credit in some way for their deliverance, which leads them to pride and other sins. Finally, the Lord humbles them through suffering under the scourge of an enemy, until they cry out to him in their humiliation and distress for deliverance.

Does this sound familiar? How often do we follow a similar pattern? Too often we try to manage life on our own, until something goes wrong. Then we beg God for help. When he provides that help, we are grateful, initially. However, with the problem solved, we often forget to pray or we do not pray well. Once again we act as if we are in control, until something goes wrong. Then we are humbled again. We need to take to heart Israel's example as a warning.

To illustrate this lesson for Israel, the Lord commands the prophet Jeremiah to do something unusual: He is to wear a loincloth for a while without washing it and then place it in the cleft of a rock. After a time Jeremiah retrieves the cloth. He discovers it is rotten and has to be thrown out. Then the Lord speaks to Jeremiah:

> Even so will I spoil the pride of Judah and the great pride of Jerusalem. This evil people, who refuse to hear my words, who stubbornly follow their own heart and have gone after other gods to serve them and worship them, shall be like this waistcloth, which is good for nothing. For as the waistcloth clings to the loins of a man, so I made the whole house of Israel and the whole house of Judah cling to me, says the LORD, that they might be for me a people,

a name, a praise, and a glory, but they would not listen.
(Jeremiah 13:9–11)

The people of God are rotting in their pride, and only the Lord in his mercy can restore them, provided they humble themselves.

THE STRENGTH OF THE HUMBLE

In contrast to the pride of many Israelites, two women exemplify a humble heart that God desires. Hannah's song, recorded in 1 Samuel 2, and Mary's *Magnificat*, recorded in Luke 1, highlight what God's strength accomplishes in a heart yielded to him. In both hymns of praise, Hannah and Mary declare that the Lord exalts those who are humble, and he humbles those who are proud, arrogant and mighty. Each understands that the child she bears is not only a gift to her but also to God's people.

Hannah prays, "My heart exults in the LORD; / my strength is exalted in the LORD / … / The bows of the mighty are broken, / but the feeble gird on strength" (1 Samuel 2:1, 4). Mary proclaims, "For he who is mighty has done great things for me, / and holy is his name. / … / He has shown strength with his arm, / he has scattered the proud in the imagination of their hearts, / … / and exalted those of low degree" (Luke 1:49, 51–52).

In both cases the Lord grants a miracle. Hannah, who has been barren for years, conceives Samuel, who becomes the last of the judges to serve as a priest in the temple and the prophet who anoints Israel's first two kings. Mary, a virgin, conceives Jesus, the Savior of the world. Each woman responds with humility for the gift she has been given.

Things are not always what they seem. Jesus' crucifixion appears to be his moment of greatest weakness, an utter humiliation, yet this is his moment of triumph. By the strength of his arms (nailed to the cross) and the strength of his Spirit, he lays down his life for us. He delivers us from the bondage to sin, taking up his life again in resurrection and then mounting to heaven in his ascension.

Consider Mary, bereft of her beloved son, helpless to intervene—at the same moment she is feeling deep agony at the death of her son, she never loses the theological virtue of joy. She participates in Jesus' self-offering as she offers her own suffering in union with his. She receives all of us as her children when Jesus gives her to the Beloved Disciple—and to each of us as beloved disciples who stand with her in the shadow of the cross, to embrace her as mother in heart and home.

Saint Paul's prayer for the Ephesians applies to us today. He prays that we will know "what is the immeasurable greatness of his power in us who believe, according to the working of his great might which he accomplished in Christ when he raised him from the dead and made him sit at his right hand in the heavenly places" (Ephesians 1:19–20).

The same power that raised Christ from the dead and enthroned him at his Father's side in heaven has been given to us. The same power of the Holy Spirit, poured out at Pentecost on his people to prepare them for their mission, is ours. And the same power we see in the lives of the saints, the deep inner strength of people who reject what the world deems as power and choose to trust in the Lord instead, has been given to us.

THE STRENGTH OF THE LORD

Strength is an attribute of God. The day King David restores the ark of the covenant to the tabernacle in Jerusalem, he declares,

> Honor and majesty are before him;
> strength and joy are in his place.
>
> Ascribe to the LORD, O families of the peoples,
> ascribe to the LORD glory and strength!
> (1 Chronicles 16:27–28)

David also refers to the Lord as strength in a psalm: "O my Strength, I will sing praises to you, / for you, O God, are my fortress, / the God who shows me mercy" (Psalm 59:17).

Later a scribe records King David's hymn of praise to God at the coronation of Solomon, shortly before David's death:

> Yours, O LORD, is the greatness, and the power, and the glory, and the victory, and the majesty; for all that is in the heavens and in the earth is yours; yours is the kingdom, O LORD, and you are exalted as head above all. Both riches and honor come from you, and you rule over all. In your hand are power and might; and in your hand it is to make great and to give strength to all. (1 Chronicles 29:11–12)

The king assures the people, through his praise for the Lord, that the Lord is *the* king, no matter who is on the throne. The Lord is the source of the king's strength.

THE LORD IS MIGHTY TO SAVE

Moses reminds Israel continually who saved them from slavery in Egypt. "By strength of hand the LORD brought us out of Egypt, from the house of bondage" (Exodus 13:14b). Following the parting of the Red Sea, Miriam leads the Israelites in this hymn: "The LORD is my strength and my song, / and he has become my salvation; / this is my God, and I will praise him, / my father's God, and I will exalt him" (Exodus 15:2). God prefaces the delivery of the Ten Commandments to Moses with, "I am the LORD your God, who brought you out of the land of Egypt, out of the house of bondage" (Exodus 20:2).

Just as the Lord brought the Israelites out of slavery into the Promised Land, so God is the one who has brought us out of slavery to sin and into the promised land of heaven. We also are dependent on God's grace for salvation:

> For by grace you have been saved through faith; and this is not your own doing, it is the gift of God—not because of works, lest any man should boast. For we are his workmanship, created in Christ Jesus for good works, which God prepared beforehand, that we should walk in them. (Ephesians 2:8–10)

By God's grace-gift we have been saved through faith. We cannot take credit for our faith, because God is the one who gave it to us as a gift; yet we must believe in order to be saved, so our faith is also an obedient response.

When we feed, clothe and contribute to a shelter that is peaceful, beautiful and orderly for our family, by the grace of God and with the gift of faith, we are walking in the good works God has prepared for us. It is grace from beginning to end as we cooperate with the gifts we have been given. To live by grace means that we admit how weak we are and how much we need his strength so that we can do these good works.

King David acknowledged that whether he was in the field watching the sheep, in battle alongside King Saul, in the wilderness fleeing from King Saul and his men or in any of the struggles he faced as king of Israel, the Lord was the source of his strength. "The LORD is my light and my salvation; whom shall I fear? The LORD is the strength of my life; of whom shall I be afraid?" (Psalm 27:1, *KJV*).

When King David returns the ark to the tabernacle, he gives the people this admonition: "Seek the LORD and his strength, / seek his presence continually!" (1 Chronicles 16:11). In other words, people of God, do not become overworked and "under-prayed," but seek his presence in his sanctuary. We know that the Lord is even more present—physically present—in the tabernacles of our sanctuaries today than he was in the tabernacle in Jerusalem. How much more should we heed King David's words and worship in his presence continually?

In another psalm David speaks about the necessity for prayer before acting. "Wait for the LORD; / be strong, and let your heart take courage; / yes, wait for the Lord!" (Psalm 27:14). It is difficult to wait; many of us would prefer a list of action steps rather than waiting. However, "prayer-less" action, in our own strength, is dangerous.

The prophet Isaiah says, "In returning and rest you shall be saved; / in quietness and in trust shall be your strength" (Isaiah 30:15). We affirm our confidence in the Lord with a simple act of faith, "Jesus, I trust in you." Our confidence is in the Lord—we are weak, but he is strong.

> He does not faint or grow weary,
>   his understanding is unsearchable.
> He gives power to the faint,
>   and to him who has no might he increases strength.
> Even youths shall faint and be weary,

and young men shall fall exhausted;
    but they who wait for the LORD shall renew their strength,
        they shall mount up with wings like eagles,
    they shall run and not be weary,
        they shall walk and not faint. (Isaiah 40:28b–31)

God delights to give us strength and we rejoice in answered prayers for increased strength.

I give you thanks, O LORD,
    with my whole heart;
    before the angels I sing your praise;
I bow down toward your holy temple
    and give thanks to your name for your mercy and
        your faithfulness;
for you have exalted above everything
    your name and your word.
On the day I called, you answered me,
    my strength of soul you increased. (Psalm 138:1–3)

We receive strength through worship. As King David proclaimed,

Blessed be the LORD!
    for he has heard the voice of my supplications.
The LORD is my strength and my shield;
    in him my heart trusts;
so I am helped, and my heart exults,
    and with my song I give thanks to him.

The LORD is the strength of his people,
    he is the saving refuge of his anointed.
…
May the LORD give strength to his people!
    May the LORD bless his people with peace!
    (Psalm 28:6–8; 29:11)

We receive strength through prayer, provided we ask the Lord for it.

HOW DO WE RELEASE GOD'S POWER IN OUR LIVES?

We need to identify what weakens us. The psalmist admits, "When I declared not my sin, my body wasted away / through my groaning all day long. / For day and night your hand was heavy upon me; / my strength was dried up as by the heat of summer" (Psalm 32:3–4). God's mercy lets us know how great our need for his strength is.

We are weakened by unconfessed sin. Sometimes we respond, "Let me clean up my mess first, and then I'll come to you, Lord." But he wants us to remember that we are very little children unable to help ourselves. We come to him in the humility of our littleness and weakness. He wants to clean us up, kiss our wounds, embrace us with his unconditional love and lead us by the hand where we need to go.

We also feel weakened by circumstances beyond our control. There are mysteries of sufferings and hardships, unrelated to our sins, which we may not understand in this life. When Saint Paul was afflicted, he begged God three times to remove the difficulty:

> But he said to me, 'My grace is sufficient for you, for my power is made perfect in weakness.' I will all the more gladly boast of my weaknesses, that the power of Christ may rest upon me. For the sake of Christ, then, I am content with weaknesses, insults, hardships, persecutions, and calamities; for when I am weak, then I am strong. (2 Corinthians 12:9–10)

God's word to Saint Paul transformed his thinking about his difficulties so that he would trust the Lord in the midst of his suffering.

Our weaknesses include our flaws, bad habits and failings. We suffer insults, founded and unfounded. We undergo hardships that are the painful consequences of our actions. We also experience persecutions, which are difficult circumstances caused by others due to our faith. And we endure calamities, which are difficult circumstances over which we have no control, and yet they have an impact on us. Regardless of the cause, we can trust the Lord to strengthen us. "And after you have suffered a little while, the God of all grace, who has called you to his eternal glory in Christ, will himself restore, establish, and strengthen you" (1 Peter 5:10).

Saint Paul chose to boast in his weakness so that God could receive glory. As he identified his weaknesses, he knew God's power would be able to work through him. He told the Corinthians, "For the foolishness of God is wiser than men, and the weakness of God is stronger than men" (1 Corinthians 1:25).

As children, a number of us sang "The Joy of the Lord Is My Strength." It is true that joy strengthens us; however, it is important to understand the context of this verse. The Israelites who had returned from exile in Babylon had just heard the book of the Law read aloud. Not only were they filled with sadness over the destruction of the temple and Jerusalem, but now they understood the extent to which *they* had broken the Law. Though they felt grief, Nehemiah urged them to focus on the joy of the Lord, for in that joy they would find the strength to return fully—body *and* soul—from captivity.

The Israelites' goal in rebuilding the temple was to worship the Lord as he desired to be worshipped. Likewise, our goal in worshipping the Lord in spirit and in truth is to glorify him as he wants to be glorified. Service done in God's strength results in glory for him, for "whoever renders service…renders it by the strength which God supplies; in order that in everything God may be glorified through Jesus Christ. To him belong glory and dominion for ever and ever. Amen" (1 Peter 4:11).

AM I WEAK ENOUGH?

Do you feel weak? God can work through you.

Do you feel weak? Then God's power can be made perfect in you.

Do you feel weak? God's grace is sufficient for you.

The psalmist admits, "My flesh and my heart may fail, / but God is the strength of my heart and my portion for ever" (Psalm 73:26). One of our weaknesses is that we do not want to admit how weak we are. We are weak, but the Lord is strong, and he will be our strength!

The critical question is *not,* am I strong enough for God to use? Rather, it is, am I weak enough? Am I totally dependent on the Lord for *his* strength to do *his* will *his* way? Through Zechariah the Lord says, "'Not by might, nor by power, but by my Spirit,' says the LORD of hosts" (Zechariah 4:6b). If we are weak, we qualify for God's power to be perfected in and through us. With Saint Paul we can say, "I can do all things in him who strengthens me" (Philippians 4:13).

CHAPTER EIGHTEEN

A Mother's Guide to the Anointing of the Sick: Strength at the Hour of Death

S uffering is inevitable in this life, but we do not have to suffer alone. The Lord will strengthen us in the midst of the trials of suffering, and he will strengthen us afterward. As the psalmist prays:

> Whom have I in heaven but you?
>> And there is nothing upon earth that I desire besides
>> you.
> My flesh and my heart may fail,
>> but God is the strength of my heart and my portion
>> for ever. (Psalm 73:25–26)

When our bodies are failing in serious illness, how do we receive God's strength?

A priest offers the Anointing of the Sick, as prescribed by Saint James: "Is any among you sick? Let him call for the elders of the Church, and let them pray over him, anointing him with oil in the name of the Lord; and the prayer of faith will save the sick man, and the Lord will raise him up; and if he has committed sins, he will be forgiven" (James 5:14–15).

On behalf of the Church, the priest commends the sick person to the grace of God, and he urges the person to unite his sufferings and prayers to Christ's passion. If the sick person is physically able and time allows, the priest offers the opportunity for Confession in preparation for receiving the Eucharist. The priest anoints him with blessed oil and prays for healing, spiritual and physical. If possible, the priest offers the opportunity for Confession in preparation for the anointing, and if possible, he offers the Eucharist as viaticum after the anointing.

On June 22, 2002, Servant of God Gwen Coniker passed away after an extended illness due to complications from a blood transfusion during a C-section delivery decades earlier. She was the mother of twelve, grandmother of fifty-four (at the time of her death) and cofounder of the Apostolate for Family Consecration with her husband, Jerry. Her son Michael wrote, "You showed us how to celebrate the gift of life, in the present moment, while balancing the sacrifices that prepare us for our final hour and doorway to eternity."[1] Gwen was a model for wives, mothers, mothers-in-law and grandmothers as she sacrificially and selflessly served her extended family and, through the apostolate, thousands of other families.

Many temptations accompany suffering, and yet there are great opportunities for us to grow spiritually and to bless others, if we will unite our sufferings to Christ's. Saint Paul testifies, "Now I rejoice in my sufferings for your sake, and in my flesh I complete what is lacking in Christ's afflictions for the sake of his body, that is, the Church" (Colossians 1:24).

Why do we pray in the rosary for grace "now and at the hour of our death"? We know we need grace now. And we know we will need special grace when we are dying.

Our suffering will not be wasted as long as we give it back to God as a gift of our weakness. We can ask him to diminish or remove our suffering, for he is our loving heavenly Father who can do all things. Yet he knows what is best for our soul's sake and for those around us, so we actively yield ourselves to him, trusting him to do what is best.

The prophet Isaiah foretold, about the Messiah, "Surely he has borne our griefs / and carried our sorrows" (Isaiah 53:4a). He not only bears our sins, but he also bears our sorrows. Jesus is Immanuel—God with us—in the midst of our agony and pain.

Saint Peter urges us to entrust our concerns to our Father, and he reminds us of the spiritual conflict that rages around us:

> Cast all your anxieties on him, for he cares about you. Be sober, be watchful. Your adversary the devil prowls around like a roaring lion, seeking some one to devour. Resist him, firm in your faith, knowing that the same experience of suffering is required of your brotherhood throughout the world. And after you have suffered a little while, the God of all grace, who has called you to his eternal glory in Christ, will himself restore, establish, and strengthen you. (1 Peter 5:7–10)

We can rest in him.

From our rebirth in Baptism to a holy death through the Anointing of the Sick, the Lord lavishes his grace on us. In addition, he enables us to serve him with the many gifts he has given us: time, talents and treasure. We are his handiwork, his beloved daughters and sons. As Saint Paul says, "And I am sure that he who began a good work in you will bring it to completion at the day of Jesus Christ" (Philippians 1:6). Whatever the challenges we face, God's grace is sufficient to strengthen us on this journey and to welcome us home.

Appendix A: Video Outlines

"She...works with willing hands."

Session One: Proverbs 31:13

I. The key to homemaking
   A. A dwelling place
      1. Psalm 90:1
      2. What makes a house a home?
   B. *A Mother's Rule of Life,* by Holly Pierlot
      1. Four similarities to a rule
      2. Four dissimilarities to a rule
II. A mother's plan of life
   A. Prayer
      1. Matthew 22:37–40
         a. All heart
         b. All soul
         c. All mind
         d. All strength
      2. "Prayer is the life of the new heart" (*CCC*, 2697).
      3. 1 Thessalonians 5:17
   B. Person
      1. Second greatest commandment
      2. "We love, because he first loved us." (1 John 4:19)
      3. How do we love ourselves?
         a. Basic physical needs (1 Corinthians 3:16–17)
         b. Emotional health and self-knowledge
         c. Mental health and family systems
         d. Be open to assistance
   C. Partner—Relationship before tasks
      1. Beloved covenant partner
      2. Vocation = call to holiness
   D. Parent
      1. Receive each child as a gift
      2. Be aware of their needs, activities, hopes for the day

      3.   Nurture with love and discipline, training and correction

      4.   Build a civilization of love in your family

  E. Provider—Our state in life

      1.   Ordinary work, extraordinary grace (Sirach 38:34)

      2.   Stewardship of resources

      3.   A nurturing atmosphere for holiness and wholeness

  F. Periphery

      1.   Catch a vision beyond our nuclear family through

          a.   hospitality

          b.   works of mercy

          c.   evangelization and missions

      2.   Plan lesser priorities lest they dominate your life

      3.   Balance between family and reaching out

III. Homemaking: A fresh perspective

  A. Face fears, failings and false notions

  B. Be mission-minded, not schedule-driven

  C. Today is a new beginning

  D. Diligence (Proverbs 4:23)

  E. Principle of stewardship (Matthew 25:21–23)

IV. "Seeks wool and flax" (Proverbs 31:13)

  A. Concerned for the practical needs of her household

  B. Clothing: best and least expensive

  C. Care for clothing

V. "Works" (Proverbs 31:13)

  A. Labor is the duty of all

  B. Labor ennobles us

  C. Proverbs 18:9

  D. Example of Tabitha (Acts 9:36–42)

VI. "With willing hands" (Proverbs 31:13)

  A. Delights in her work

  B. Cooperates with grace (Philippians 4:13)

  C. Works skillfully (1 Samuel 2:18–21)

VII. Mother's guide to the sacraments: Baptism

  A. God covers Adam and Eve's nakedness (Genesis 3:21)

B. God covers our spiritual nakedness (Galatians 3:27)

C. In Baptism we "put on" Christ

D. Warning (1 Peter 3:20–21)

"She...provides food for her household."

SESSION TWO: PROVERBS 31:15

I. Food is a gift from the Lord
   A. Plants (Genesis 1:29)
   B. Meat (Genesis 9:3)
   C. A Proverbs 31 woman's attitude combines faith and work
      1. Psalm 145:15
      2. Don't be anxious. (Matthew 6:25–27, 31–34)
   D. Plan ahead

II. Gathers food
   A. Fresh ingredients
   B. Enterprising spirit
   C. Profitable exchanges
   D. Variety of food
   E. Thoughtfulness to detail (Proverbs 21:5)

III. Comfort food
   A. The original comfort food, breast milk
   B. Comfort—"come" and "strengthen"; role of the Holy Spirit
   C. Taste associated with loving care (Sirach 26:13)
   D. Care communicated through homemade food
   E. Ethnic foods
   F. Creative leftovers

IV. Prepares the food
   A. Simplify shopping with rotating menu
   B. Be creative; one new recipe each week
   C. Adjust for seasons
   D. Adjust for liturgical fasting and feasting
   E. Apply the fruit of the Spirit while preparing food (Galatians 5:22–23)
   F. Wonderful smells
   G. Cooking with children
   H. *Once-a-Month Cooking* or *Dinner's in the Freezer*

V. Serves the food
   A. The importance of the dining room
   B. Beauty in table setting

    c.   Family meals

    d.   Private or public blessings

        1.   Gather for thanksgiving

        2.   Meaningful communication (Proverbs 17:1)

        3.   Healing can happen: love and laughter; no negative humor

    e.   Snacks

    f.   Hospitality—entertain angels unaware (Hebrews 13:2)

    g.   Attitude of graciousness—Martha (Luke 10:38–42; John 12:1–3)

vi. Feeding the hunger of the heart

    a.   Language of love

    b.   Why do we eat?

        1.   Communion

        2.   Celebration

        3.   Pleasure

        4.   To sustain our lives

    c.   What am I hungry for? Don't substitute food for love

    d.   Weight challenges

        1.   Battling my body or uniting my mind and body?

        2.   Greater self-control

        3.   Health

    e.   Food is a gift (Romans 14:13–21)

    f.   Eat and drink to the glory of God! (1 Corinthians 10:31)

vii. A mother's guide to the sacraments: the Eucharist

    a.   Old Testament: Passover (see Exodus 12:5–13) New Testament: Christ (1 Corinthians 10:7–8)

    b.   Old Testament manna: Heavenly daily bread (Exodus 16:14–15) New Testament: Jesus is the bread from heaven (John 6:48–51)

    c.   Old Testament: *Todah* (Psalm 50:14–15) New Testament: The Eucharist is our *Todah* (Luke 22:19–20)

"She rises while it is yet night."

SESSION THREE: PROVERBS 31:15A

I. Gift of time

    A. We were made to live forever (Galatians 2:20)

    B. Eternity in man's mind (Ecclesiastes 3:11)

    C. *Now* is the moment eternity touches our lives

II. She rises early

    A. Prayer in the morning

        1. Lamentations 3:21–24

        2. Specific time (Proverbs 26:14)

        3. Specific location (Luke 4:42)

        4. Specific materials

    B. God's blessing on our work (Proverbs 16:3)

    C. Commit plans to the Lord of time

    D. Distractions and interruptions

    E. Jesus' example (Luke 22:42)

    F. Pray throughout the day (Ephesians 6:18)

III. Priority loving leads to priority living

    A. Prayer—get bearings before bombardment

        1. Time for prayer

        2. Time for receiving the sacraments

        3. Time to grow in knowledge of the Faith

        4. Balance

    B. Person—physical needs

        1. Sleep

        2. Proper nutrition

        3. Overall health, including exercise (Sirach 30:15, 16)

    C. Partner

        1. Time for communion

        2. Time for union

    D. Parent

        1. Unconditional love

        2. Enjoy time together: eat, work, play, pray

        3. Love languages

IV. Provider—establish a schedule
    A. Planner as a tool
    B. File folders for paper management
    C. Weekly pattern of family life recorded
       1. Group tasks
       2. Schedule regular activities.
       3. Sunday as the Lord's Day
       4. Saturday as the day of preparation
       5. Family meeting for needs, tasks, appointments and so on
    D. Other uses for your planner
V. Manage schedule
    A. Disorder is more limiting than a schedule
    B. Uncluttered time and space lead to uncluttered thinking.
    C. Mortification: doing what I don't want to do when I need to
    D. Working together as a team
    E. *Organizing Time From the Inside Out*
       1. Set goals: long-term, short-term. *SMART*—
           *S*pecific
           *M*easurable
           *A*ction-oriented
           *R*ealistic
           *T*imely
    F. Time for weekly planning
    G. Nightly fifteen minutes to review the next day
       1. Letters *A, B, C, D, E*
           *A*ct today!
           *B*est if I could do it today
           *C*ould do it this week, if able
           *D*elegate to someone else
           *E*liminate—not my job to do
       2. Add numbers to prioritize jobs in each letter
       3. Take plan to prayer in the morning for further insight
VI. Seasons of life
    A. Sense of failure, what to do?
    B. A time for everything (Ecclesiastes 3:1–8)

c. Adjust for temporary imbalances

d. Submit schedule to the Lord

e. "Yes, Lord!" (Colossians 3:23–24)

VII. Time wasters

    A. Unclear goals (Luke 14:28–30)

    B. Lack of planning (Proverbs 20:4)

    C. Unclear family rules

    D. Lack of order

    E. Procrastination (Proverbs 14:23)

    F. Misplaced priorities (Proverbs 28:19)

    G. Interruptions

    H. Life challenges

VIII. A mother's guide to the sacraments: Confirmation

    A. Strengthened by the Spirit to be witnesses (Acts 1:8)

    B. Sealed with the Spirit (Ephesians 1:13–14)

    C. Gifted by the Spirit (Isaiah 11:2): Jesus; us
       Gifts of the Holy Spirit: wisdom, understanding, counsel,
          fortitude, knowledge, fear of the Lord, piety

    D. Jesus made choices about time

    E. Saint Augustine, Saint Gregory the Great, Saint Thomas
       Aquinas

    F. Time management and the Spirit's gifts

IX. We need to press on (Philippians 3:12–14).

"She...provides...tasks for her maidens."

SESSION FOUR: PROVERBS 31:15B

I. The beginning of the day
 A. Caring for needs sets the tone of the day
 B. Prioritizing people before tasks
 C. Knowing limits and what others can do to assist
 D. Providing structure for the day (Sirach 26:16)

II. Genius of woman
 A. Different from men; primarily relational
 B. Tasks have a specific bent: "in relation to"
 C. Like the Holy Spirit (Genesis 1:1–2)

III. Called to be a keeper of the home
 A. Adam and Eve to guard the garden (Genesis 2:15)
 B. Various Old Testament keepers
 C. The Lord is our keeper (Psalm 121:5–8)
 D. Called to be housekeepers

IV. Housework is God's work
 A. Maintaining a sense of humor
 B. Drawing from a reservoir of grace (Hebrews 4:15–16)
 C. Remember for whom we work: the Lord
  Little things done with great love
 D. Cleaning is a big part of the little things we do
 E. Biblical concept of cleansing
  1. Set apart for godly use
  2. God cleanses his people from sin

V. Home is a place of order
 A. A place prepared for you (John 14:2–3)
 B. How do we prepare a room?
  1. Think through each space; *Organizing from the Inside Out*
  2. Primary function of each area of the room
  3. Beauty in the room
 C. What will it take to maintain this space?
  1. Clutter management
  2. Family management
  3. Cleaning management; *Sidetracked Home Executives*

VI. Home is a place of beauty
   A. Sanctuary (Psalm 27:4)
   B. Role of beauty (Ezra 7:27)
   C. Nurturing life (Proverbs 24:3–4)
   D. Detachment

VII. Home is a place of peace and safety
   A. God is your dwelling place (Deuteronomy 33:27a)
      A place of safety and rest, a harbor
   B. God is our refuge; he is a haven (Psalm 61:3–4)
      1. Conflict resolution, a sanctuary. *Chosen and Cherished*
      2. Ambiance: light and sound

VIII. Do we feel competent in homemaking?
   A. Prepared?
   B. How do we become more competent?
   C. Older women as mentors (Titus 2:3–5)
   D. Teachable spirit
   E. Evaluate the cost of disorganization
   F. Cooperate with grace in humility and gratitude

IX. A renewed vision for homemaking
   A. What homemaking is not versus what it is
   B. The value of a hidden life
   C. Complementarity with your spouse
   D. Family's attitudes toward your work

X. Tasks for maidens
   A. Who helps you? Children, your homegrown team!
   B. Have a well-thought-out plan
   C. Delegate as a good steward of their time

XI. A mother's guide to the sacraments: Confession
   A. Sins committed after Baptism (James 5:16)
   B. He will forgive (1 John 1:9).
   C. Why confess to a priest? (Sirach 34:25–26)
   D. How often should we go? (Romans 7:19)
      Mortal sins and venial sins (1 John 5:16–17)
   E. Contrition perfected; grace of absolution received—penance
   F. We have damaged the whole body of Christ—reparation
   G. Whatever takes a whack at pride is a step in the right direction!

"She considers a field and buys it;
with the fruit of her hands, she plants a vineyard."

SESSION FIVE: PROVERBS 31:16

I. Planted in a garden
   A. Adam and Eve called to subdue the earth (Genesis 1:28).
   B. Adam and Eve called to till and keep the garden (Genesis 2:15).
   C. Consequence of the Fall: thorns, increased pain in labor

II. Land is a gift
   A. Noah (Genesis 9:20)
   B. Abraham (Genesis 12:1–3)
   C. Moses (Deuteronomy 28:1–4, 15–16, 18)
   D. David and the Holy of Holies garden imagery
   E. Garden or desert?

III. The Proverbs 31 woman is a dominion woman
   A. "She considers a field"
      1. Prudent with resources
      2. Desire to expand boundaries (1 Chronicles 4:10)
   B. "and buys it"
      1. Industrious
      2. Prepares for the future; *The Total Money Makeover*
   C. "with the fruit of her hands"
      1. Family earnings
      2. Work with your children
      3. Let the land give glory to God
   D. "She plants a vineyard"
      1. She subdues the earth through hands-on involvement
      2. She tills and keeps the garden

IV. Lessons from the Old Testament
   A. It takes time (Leviticus 19:23–25)
   B. The land's Sabbath rest (Leviticus 25:2–4)
   C. Break up fallow ground (Hosea 10:12)
   D. Deeply rooted tree or wind-driven chaff? (Psalm 1:1–4)
   E. Desolation in God's vineyard (Isaiah 5:7, 9)
   F. God can make a desert bloom (Isaiah 44:3)
   G. God's Word as seed will bear fruit (Isaiah 55:10–11)

v. Lessons from the New Testament

    A. John 15:1–6, 9–11

        1. Stay connected

        2. If connected, you will bear fruit

        3. Pruning is a given

        4. Fullness of joy

    B. Matthew 13:18–23

        1. Seed sown along the path (vv. 18, 19)

        2. Seed sown on rocky ground (vv. 20, 21)

        3. Seed sown among thorns (v. 22)

        4. Seed sown on good soil (v. 23)

    C. Matthew 7:15–20

    D. Galatians 6:7–8

vi. Cultivating contemplation

    A. Monasteries

    B. Psalm 128:2

    C. Sirach 7:15

    D. *The Hidden Art of Homemaking*

    E. Sins can be the great mulch of life!

vii. Tend the garden

    A. From plants in pots to plots of farmland—eleven steps

    B. The garden within—eleven steps

viii. A mother's guide to the sacraments: Holy Orders and Holy Matrimony

    A. Both

        1. Our mission in life = vocation to love

        2. Reflect the life-giving power of self-donating love (God)

        3. Nothing less than 100 percent (the lordship of Jesus Christ)

        4. God does not call you to what you do not want to do (free consent).

        5. We need grace to be faithful to his call

        6. Grace is available to make us fruitful

    B. Unique

        1. Marriage reflects the relationship between Christ and the Church

        2. Priest is *in persona Christi*

        3. Religious life: women choose Jesus as their groom

"She clothes her loins with strength and makes her arms strong."

SESSION SIX: PROVERBS 31:17

I. Proverbs 31:17
   A. She prepares for her work (Psalm 65:6; 93:1–2)
   B. She makes her arms strong (Deuteronomy 6:4–5; Psalm 144:12)

II. Five tasks for which people gird their loins
   A. With strength for battle (Psalm 18:31–32, 39; 33:16–19; 68:34–35; Ephesians 6:10–18a; 1 John 4:4)
   B. With inner courage to face trials (Joshua 1:9; Job 38:3); Saint Paul (2 Timothy 1:7–8; 2:15; 4:17a); Saint Peter (1 Peter 1:13)
   C. Vested for priestly service—kingdom of priests (Exodus 19:5–6; 29:9; Revelation 1:5b–6); a prophetic role (Jeremiah 1:17)
   D. To prepare for repentance (Psalm 30:11–12; Jeremiah 4:8; Joel 1:13–15)
   E. To work diligently: Passover (Exodus 12:11); faithful servants (Luke 12:35–37); Jesus' example (John 13:4–5)

III. The strength of the proud
   A. God humbles the proud (Job 12:13, 21b)
   B. Cycle throughout the book of Judges

IV. The strength of the humble
   A. Thanksgiving for a child
     1. Hannah's song (1 Samuel 2:1a, 4)
     2. Echoed in Mary's *Magnificat* (Luke 1:49, 51)
   B. Jesus' crucifixion
     1. Jesus
     2. Mary
   C. Jesus' resurrection (Ephesians 1:19–20)
   D. The Holy Spirit at Pentecost
   E. The saints

V. The strength of the Lord
   A. Strength is an attribute of God (1 Chronicles 16:27–28; 29:10–13; Psalm 59:17)
   B. God alone saves us

  1. Moses (Exodus 13:14b; 15:2)

  2. David (Psalm 118:14)

  3. Saint Paul (Ephesians 2:8–10)

 C. To live by grace, we admit weakness (1 Chronicles 16:11; Psalm 27:14; Isaiah 30:15; 40:28b–31)

 D. God delights to give us strength (Psalm 28:6–8)

VI. How do we release God's strength in our lives?

 A. What weakens us?

  1. Unconfessed sin (Psalm 32:3–4)

  2. Suffering (2 Corinthians 12:9–10)

   a. Weaknesses

   b. Insults

   c. Hardships

   d. Persecutions

   e. Calamities

 B. What strengthens us?

  1. Saint Paul boasts in weakness

  2. Weak enough to be useful?

  3. God's power perfected in weakness

  4. His Spirit (Zechariah 4:6b)

  5. His joy (Nehemiah 8:10b)

  6. Strength God supplies (1 Peter 4:11)

  7. Philippians 4:13

VII. A mother's guide to the sacraments: Anointing of the Sick

 A. Now and at the hour of our death

 B. Prayer for healing

 C. Psalm 73:25–26

 D. 1 Peter 5:6–11

VIII. Conclusion of series study (Colossians 1:9–12)

Appendix B:
Questions for an Intergenerational Women's Study

Session One: *"She...works with willing hands."*

1. What do you hope to get out of this study?
2. What do you think about the framework of a plan of life? Is there anything you would add to or remove from this plan?
3. What's the difference between being mission-minded and being schedule-driven in relation to the tasks of homemaking? Have you ever set aside your schedule, realizing it was taking you away from your mission? What were the results?
4. Have you thought about how much food, sleep and exercise you need? How might your life and your family's life be different if these elements of your life worked better?
5. What does success in the vocation of marriage look like? How do you measure it?
6. How can you get the grace to do God's will in his strength? Name practical and spiritual strategies for receiving that grace.
7. How can you utilize your gifts better in your homemaking?
8. What skills do you hope your daughter(s) will learn?
9. Read 2 Thessalonians 3:6–13. How might this passage apply to homemaking?
10. Did you receive any training or advice from your mother or grandmother regarding clothing, such as how to sew or how to dress modestly yet stylishly? How do you intend to pass on your skills and insights regarding clothing to your daughter(s)?
11. What resource has benefited you the most?
12. How can you grow in your appreciation for the grace of Baptism in your life?

SESSION TWO: *"She...provides food for her household."*

1. Name one fresh insight regarding food that you received from this study. How will that insight impact your care for your family?

2. How important were family meals to you growing up? Were they a daily or nearly daily part of your family life? How do you feel about your family's approach to the family meal, and what effect do you think that approach had on strengthening or weakening family ties?

3. As a child, how important was food in celebrating holidays or birthdays?

4. How important are family meals to you now? Are there any changes you can make so that your family meals become occasions of even greater mutual support and warmth?

5. What training in cooking or baking did you receive from your mother? From your grandmother or another significant woman in your life? What resource has benefited you the most in the area of cooking?

6. What have you done to increase your skills in the area of cooking?

7. How do you bring elements of the liturgical calendar into your meals?

8. What can you do—or what have you done—to bring elements of the liturgical calendar into your meals? What resources help you to do that? How does your family respond to these meal-centered reminders of the liturgical calendar?

9. How can you prepare yourself and your loved ones for receiving the Eucharist?

10. What is the relationship between Communion at Mass and your sense of communion in your family?

SESSION THREE: *"She rises while it is yet night."*

1. Do you find it limits you to set a schedule or use a planner? If so, why? Is there any way in which a schedule or planner might be of value to you?

2. What is currently working well for you in the area of personal prayer, and how can you balance time in prayer with time spent on tasks?

3. How important is it to you to take care of yourself? How do you know when you've crossed into either selfishness or failure to take proper care of yourself?

4. Do you spend more time on the relationships in your family or on the tasks of homemaking? How can you achieve a better balance?

5. What does it mean that homemaking involves an "apostolate of interruption"? And how can you limit unnecessary interruptions?

6. What limitations do you foresee in following your plan of life? How can you adjust the plan for *this* season of your life?

7. What are some of your time wasters?

8. Have you and your spouse set goals together to fulfill the dreams you share for financial freedom? For caring for your children? For growing closer to each other in your family? For serving the Lord? Would your spouse be willing to work with you to set long-range goals and plan how they can be achieved?

9. Is there one resource that has helped you the most with time management and that you recommend to others?

10. Time management is a challenge when a woman is home full-time with her first baby. What suggestions do you have to help a young mother manage her time well?

11. How can the gifts of the Spirit (see Isaiah 11:2) we receive through Confirmation help us with time management?

SESSION FOUR: *"She...provides...tasks for her maidens."*

1. What aspect of homemaking has been easy for you? Difficult for you?
2. Based on a renewed vision for what you are called to do, how do you need to adjust your perspective?
3. Does your husband value your homemaking work? If not, how can you help him understand the tasks that make up your day, as well as the value of your "ministry of presence"?
4. What did his mother do or not do that he hopes you will either imitate or not do in the area of homemaking?
5. Consider the key women in your life when you were growing up. What did they do regarding homemaking that you want to imitate? What do you not want to imitate?
6. Did you receive any training in housekeeping when you were growing up? What do you wish you had been taught?
7. What resource would you recommend about homemaking?
8. How have you come to understand ordinary tasks in a spiritual way? How has this helped you appreciate these tasks more and perform them better?
9. What are some practical things you can do to establish a habit of regular Confession?

SESSION FIVE: *"She considers a field and buys it;*
with the fruit of her hands, she plants a vineyard."

1. What does it mean that land is a gift? What does your "land" consist of at this point in your life?

2. How does the Proverbs 31 woman manage her land? How can you help the land give glory to God?

3. Were you involved in gardening or farming as a child? If so, did that experience instill in you any interest in gardening? How did it influence your ideas about God and nature?

4. Have you planted a garden as an adult? If not, how might you begin? If so, has your gardening deepened your relationship with God?

5. Can you see any ways in which the warnings in the Old and New Testament teachings about the connection between fruitfulness and obedience apply in your life?

6. How can you stay connected to Jesus so that your life bears fruit? Think about a time when you felt "disconnected." How did you restore that relationship with Jesus? Did you see some good fruit as a result of your return to the Lord?

7. What are the parallels between cultivating a garden and cultivating your spiritual life? How can you improve the soil of your soul so that God's Word can take deep root in your life?

8. How does grace enable someone to be faithful and fruitful, spiritually and physically, through one of the sacraments of consecration, Holy Orders or Holy Matrimony? What does this grace look like in your own life?

SESSION SIX: *"She clothes her loins with strength
and makes her arms strong."*

1. What is the difference between depending on the Lord for his strength and trying to do something on your own? How have you experienced this difference in your own life?

2. How does Mary exemplify strength in humility? Has there been a specific occasion when Mary's example directly affected a choice that you made?

3. What does it mean to love God with "all your might"? Is there a person or saint whose example in this regard has particularly inspired you?

4. What weakens you in the midst of your vocation of marriage? How is "God's strength made perfect in your weakness"? What impact does that have on your relationship with God?

5. What strengthens you in your vocation?

6. How can you offer your sufferings as a gift to God? What fruit have you seen as a result of offering your sufferings to God?

7. Are you aware of spiritual warfare in the midst of ordinary life? How can you equip your children for spiritual warfare without creating anxiety or fear in them?

8. In the Hail Mary, why do we pray for grace "at the hour of our death"?

9. How does the Anointing of the Sick prepare us for heaven?

APPENDIX C:
Key Questions for Buying Your Next Home

Address: _____ Cost: _____

Year built: _____ How long on the market? _____

Lot size: _____ Phone # of contact _____

Living Room: size _____ colors _____
- ❏ closet ❏ carpet ❏ hardwood
- ❏ wood-burning fireplace ❏ gas fireplace
- ❏ bay window ❏ drapes ❏ ceiling fan

Dining Room: size _____ colors _____
- ❏ pantry ❏ off kitchen ❏ separate from kitchen
- ❏ carpet ❏ hardwood ❏ drapes ❏ ceiling fan

Kitchen: size _____ colors _____
type/number of cabinets _____
- ❏ carpet ❏ hardwood ❏ tile ❏ linoleum
- ❏ table area ❏ dishwasher ❏ oven ❏ disposal
- ❏ refrigerator ❏ microwave ❏ water purifier ❏ fan(s)

Family Room: size _____ colors _____
- ❏ carpet ❏ hardwood ❏ shelves ❏ ceiling fan

Bathroom(s): # full _____ # partial _____

size _____ _____ _____

colors _____ _____ _____

flooring _____ _____ _____

closets, shelving _____ _____ _____

fan(s) _____ _____ _____

Bedrooms:

size _____ _____ _____

colors _____ _____ _____

flooring _____ _____ _____

shelving _____ _____ _____

special features _____ _____ _____

drapes _____ _____ _____

Sun Room? _____

Attic: flooring _____
❑ finished   ❑ whole house fan

Basement: flooring _____
How is house heated? _____
age of hot water heater _____   age of furnace _____
❑ finished   ❑ water in the basement
❑ washer   ❑ dryer   ❑ freezer   ❑ crawl space
❑ asbestos   ❑ water softener ❑ air-conditioning

Garage: ❑ attached   ❑ 1 car   ❑ 2 cars

Roof: age _____ material _____ gutters, soffits age _____

Yard:
❑ level   ❑ inclined   ❑ trees
❑ fencing   ❑ play equipment

Patio/Deck: size _____ condition _____

Windows:
❑ thermal   ❑ triple-track   ❑ put in storms each year
❑ insulation

Average Bills: electric _____   water _____
                         gas _____   garbage _____
                         property taxes _____

Other special features (fireplaces and so on)

_____
_____
_____
_____
_____
_____
_____

Appendix D:
Making a House a Home, Room by Room

Imagination:

Room or closet to be organized _____   Date _____

What is the primary purpose for this room?

What are possible secondary uses?

Observation:

What is working right now or at least partly working?

What needs to change? Standing in the room, I can see these problems:
I can never find

_____.

I need a place for

_____.

There's no room for

_____.

I want to change

_____.

In this room, I no longer need

_____.

Due to the clutter or room arrangement, I can't

_____.

Organization Plan:

Divide the room into areas for specific purposes:

Major Purpose	Furniture & Supplies Needed for each Area	Storage Required
_____	_____	_____
_____	_____	_____
_____	_____	_____

Sketch space on a blank piece of paper: Measure the room's dimensions, including ceiling height.

- Note plugs & phone jacks
- Place doors, windows, radiators and any other permanent fixtures
- Note architectural features
- Is there any major work needed: Electrical? Plumbing? Carpentry? Building or tearing down?

Place furniture where you would like it; designate storage spaces.

Implementation:
Contact any professionals needed for major work.
Gather boxes:
> Throw out, Give away, Belongs elsewhere, Something "To Do"
> In a clockwise direction, sort stuff into these boxes or set aside to place in the room.

Designate a room in which you'll temporarily place furniture & items no longer needed here.

> Place furniture you want in the arrangement that fits the purposes for the room.
> What containers are needed to keep items in their proper paces, considering aesthetics?
> Put those containers—storage bins, shelves or furniture—in place.
> Assign a place for each item that fit the purposes of the room.

Gather items from the rest of the house that fits the room's purposes.

Note decorating ideas (paint, wallpaper, stenciling, fabric, flooring):

Note needed repairs:

Note specific cleaning and maintenance instructions:

BIBLIOGRAPHY

BOOKS

Aslett, Don. *Clutter's Last Stand: It's Time to De-Junk Your Life!*
Cincinnati: Writer's Digest, 1984.

Catechism of the Catholic Church. Vatican City: Libreria Editrice
Vaticana, 1994.

Chapman, Gary. *The Five Love Languages: How to Express Heartfelt
Commitment to Your Mate.* Chicago: Northfield, 1995.

_____ and Ross Campbell. *The Five Love Languages of Children.*
Chicago: Moody, 1997.

Cilley, Marla. *Sink Reflections.* New York: Bantam, 2002.

Cruise, Jorge. *8 Minutes in the Morning: A Simple Way to Shed Up to
2 Pounds a Week Guaranteed.* New York: Harper Collins, 2001.

Cunningham, Sally Jean. *Great Garden Companions: A Companion
Planting System for a Beautiful, Chemical-Free Vegetable Garden.*
Emmaus, Pa.: Rodale, 1998.

Escrivá, Josemaría. *The Way.* New York: Random House, 2006.

Felton, Sandra. *Organizing Magic: 40 Days to a Well-Ordered Home
and Life.* Grand Rapids, Mich.: Revell, 2006.

_____. *The Messies Manual: The Procrastinator's Guide to Good
Housekeeping.* Grand Rapids, Mich.: Revell, 1983.

_____. *When You Live with a Messie.* Grand Rapids, Mich.: Revell,
1994.

Gesto, Katie. *Bulimia: Hunger for Freedom—My Spiritual Journey of
Recovery.* Longwood, Fla.: Xulon, 2004.

Hahn, Kimberly K. *Chosen and Cherished: Biblical Wisdom for Your
Marriage.* Cincinnati: Servant, 2007.

_____. *Life-Giving Love: Embracing God's Beautiful Design for
Marriage.* Cincinnati: Servant, 2001.

Hahn, Scott W. *The Lamb's Supper: The Mass as Heaven on Earth.*
New York: Doubleday, 1999.

_____. *Ordinary Work, Extraordinary Grace: My Spiritual Journey
in Opus Dei.* New York: Doubleday, 2006.

_____. *Swear to God: The Promise and the Power of the Sacraments.*
New York: Doubleday, 2004.

_____, and Kimberly Hahn. *Rome Sweet Home: Our Journey to Catholicism.* San Francisco: Ignatius, 1993.

_____, and Leon J. Suprenant, eds. *Catholic for a Reason: Scripture and the Mystery of the Family of God.* Steubenville, Ohio: Emmaus Road, 1998.

_____, and Regis J. Flaherty, eds. *Catholic for a Reason IV: Scripture and the Mystery of Marriage and Family Life.* Steubenville, Ohio: Emmaus Road, 2007.

Kinecke, Genevieve. *The Authentic Catholic Woman.* Cincinnati: Servant, 2006.

Kolberg, Judith, and Kathleen Nadeau. *ADD-Friendly Ways to Organize Your Life.* New York: Brunner-Routledge, 2002.

Lenahan, Phil. *7 Steps to Becoming Financially Free: A Catholic Guide to Managing Your Money.* Huntington, Ind.: Our Sunday Visitor, 2006.

Martin, Michaelann, Carol Puccio and Zoe Romanowsky. *The Catholic Parent Book of Feasts: Celebrating the Church Year With Your Family.* Huntington, Ind.: Our Sunday Visitor, 1999.

Martinez, Susie, Vanda Howell and Bonnie Garcia. *Don't Panic— Dinner's in the Freezer: Great-Tasting Meals You Can Make Ahead.* Grand Rapids, Mich.: Revell, 2005.

McCoy, Jonni. *Miserly Moms: Living on One Income in a Two-Income Economy.* Elkton, Md.: Full Quart, 1996.

McElhone, James F. *Particular Examen.* Notre Dame, Ind.: Ave Maria, 1952.

Morgenstern, Julie. *Organizing from the Inside Out: The Foolproof System of Organizing Your Home, Your Office and Your Life.* New York: Henry Holt, 1998.

_____. *Time Management from the Inside Out: The Foolproof System for Taking Control of Your Schedule—and Your Life.* New York: Henry Holt, 2004.

Parsons, Rob. *The 60 Minute Marriage Builder: An Hour of Reading for a Lifetime of Love.* Nashville: Broadman and Holman, 1998.

Pierlot, Holly. *A Mother's Rule of Life: How to Bring Order to Your Home and Peace to Your Soul.* Manchester, N.H.: Sophia, 2004.

Ramsey, Dave. *The Total Money Makeover: A Proven Plan for Financial Fitness.* Nashville: Nelson, 2007.

Scanlan, Michael. *Appointment with God.* Steubenville, Ohio: Franciscan University Press, 1987.

Schaeffer, Edith. *The Hidden Art of Homemaking.* Wheaton, Ill.: Tyndale, 1971.

Trapp, Maria Augusta. *Around the Year with the Trapp Family: Keeping the Feasts and Seasons of the Christian Year.* New York: Pantheon, 1955.

Van Zeller, Hubert. *Holiness for Housewives: And Other Working Women* (reprinted and abridged). Manchester, N.H.: Sophia, 1997.

Vitz, Evelyn Birge. *A Continual Feast: A Cookbook to Celebrate the Joys of Family and Faith throughout the Christian Year.* New York: Ignatius, 1999.

Weaver, Joanna. *Having a Mary Heart in a Martha World: Finding Intimacy With God in the Busyness of Life.* Colorado Springs: WaterBrook, 2000.

Wilson, Mimi, and Mary Beth Lagerborg. *Once-a-Month Cooking: A Proven System for Spending Less Time in the Kitchen and Enjoying Delicious, Homemade Meals Every Day* (revised and expanded). New York: St. Martin's, 2007.

Young, Pamela I., and Peggy A. Jones. *Sidetracked Home Executives: From Pigpen to Paradise.* New York: Warner, 2001.

INTERNET SOURCES

All Recipes (www.allrecipes.com). More than forty thousand recipes available for free; can adjust for any number of persons.

Domestic-Church.com (www.domestic-church.com). Resources to assist families in living the liturgical calendar in their homes.

Fish Eaters (www.fisheaters.com/marygardens.html). Ideas for Mary Gardens.

FlyLady.net (www.FlyLady.net). Daily words of encouragement and suggestions for "sidetracked home executives," to help organize their homes.

Gardens Ablaze (www.gardensablaze.com/companions/companions.htm).
    Ideas for establishing companion gardens.
The Light Weigh (www.lightweigh.com). A combination weight-loss
    program and spiritual enrichment program by Suzanne Fowler.
Mary's Gardens (www.mgardens.org). Explanations of the various
    flowers renamed during medieval times for the Blessed Virgin
    Mary.
Messies Anonymous: Home of the Organizer Lady
    (www.messies.com). Organization founded by Sandra Felton for
    anyone who has difficulty getting and staying organized.
Recipezaar (www.recipezaar.com). List ingredients you have at home,
    and you'll be offered a recipe—ideal when you cannot get to the
    store that day. If you find a recipe you like, you can add it to a
    cookbook collection the Web site creates for you. All of this is free.
Taste of Home (www.tasteofhome.com). Tips and recipes from expe-
    rienced home cooks.
Weight Watchers (www.weightwatchers.com). More than forty years
    of experience helping people lose weight; free trial available for
    the online program.

PRESENTATION
Kiser, Tami. "Smart Martha Seminars" on home organization, avail-
    able at conferences around the country. For more information,
    go to www.smartmartha.com.

VIDEO SERIES
Hahn, Kimberly. *Life-Nurturing Love Series* in four installments of six
    Bible studies each. The first set of six studies is entitled *Chosen
    and Cherished: Biblical Wisdom for Your Marriage.* The second set
    of six studies has the same title as this book, *Graced and Gifted:
    Biblical Wisdom for a Homemaker's Heart.* For more information
    contact Servant Books, 800-488-0488.

NOTES

PART ONE: *She Works With Willing Hands*

CHAPTER ONE: *Priority Loving Leads to Priority Living*

1. Edith Schaeffer writes, "Of course, human relationships make a house into a home: either the relationships within the house, or the welcome and understanding that guests find." *The Hidden Art of Homemaking* (Wheaton, Ill.: Tyndale, 1971), p. 99.
2. "The ABC of Rules of Life" by Pete Greig; *The Order of the Mustard Seed,* available at www.mustardseedorder.com/cm/home/9.
3. Holly Pierlot, subtitle of her book, *A Mother's Rule of Life: How to Bring Order to Your Home and Peace to Your Soul.*
4. St. Joseph Communications has hundreds of talks and audio-books available.
5. See my chapter entitled "The World After the Wedding" in Scott Hahn and Regis J. Flaherty, eds., *Catholic for a Reason IV: Scripture and the Mystery of Marriage and Family Life* (Steubenville, Ohio: Emmaus Road, 2007), pp. 17–28.
6. Please see the next book in the *Life-Nurturing Love* series for more details.
7. Quoted in Gwen C. Coniker, *Love… is Patient, …is Kind, …Never Ends: A compilation of writings and talks by Gwen Coniker and those who knew and loved her* (Bloomingdale, Ohio: Apostolate for Family Consecration), p. 107.

CHAPTER TWO: *Ordinary Work, Extraordinary Grace*

1. Pure Fashion's Web address is www.purefashion.com.
2. Translation is from the *New American Bible* (New York: P.J. Kenedy, 1970).

CHAPTER THREE: *A Mother's Guide to Baptism*

1. See my chapter "Born Again: What the Bible Teaches About Baptism" in Scott Hahn and Leon J. Suprenant, *Catholic for a Reason: Scripture and the Mystery of the Family of God* (Steubenville, Ohio: Emmaus Road, 1998), pp. 113–138.

PART TWO: *She Brings Her Food From Afar*

CHAPTER FOUR: *She Provides Food for Her Household*

1. www.allrecipes.com.
2. Susie Martinez, Vanda Howell and Bonnie Garcia's *Don't Panic—Dinner's in the Freezer: Great-Tasting Meals You Can Make Ahead* (Grand Rapids, Mich.: Revell, 2005) has a very similar concept and is also an excellent reference.
3. Schaeffer, p. 123.

CHAPTER FIVE: *Feeding the Hunger of the Heart*

1. Six percent of anorexics are men. See Dr. Barton Blinder, "Anorexia in Males," www.ltspeed.com.
2. See Katie Gesto, *Bulimia: Hunger for Freedom—My Spiritual Journey of Recovery* (Longwood, Fla.: Xulon, 2004).
3. See Peggy Claude-Pierre, *The Secret Language of Eating Disorders: How You Can Understand and Work to Cure Anorexia and Bulimia* (New York: Crown, 1997).
4. This is not a paid endorsement. Weight Watchers—particularly my leader, Judy—has been a great blessing in my life and I want to share about it as a personal note.
5. Josemaría Escrivá, *The Way* (New York: Random House, 2006), p. 57, no. 172.
6. Escrivá, p. 59, no. 179.

PART THREE: *She Rises While It Is Still Night*

CHAPTER SEVEN: *Rhythm of Life: The Dance of Time Management*

1. Escrivá, p. 61, no. 191.
2. *Magnificat*, a monthly pocket-size publication, contains morning and evening prayers and daily Mass readings. Every cover is an attractive work of art. See www.magnificat.com. Highly recommended.

3. *The Word Among Us* offers inspirational articles and one-page meditations on daily Mass readings. See www.wau.org. Highly recommended.

4. See Mother Teresa and Brian Kolodiejchuk, *Mother Teresa: Come Be My Light: The Private Writings of the Saint of Calcutta* (New York: Doubleday, 2007).

5. As a child Saint Josemaría Escrivá learned this beautiful prayer from a pious priest.

6. For more information contact the St. Paul Center for Biblical Theology, www.salvationhistory.com.

7. For more information go to www.greatadventureonline.com.

8. Emmaus Road Publishing has studies by Stacy Mitch, Michaelann Martin, Curtis Martin, Tim Gray, Ted Sri and Michael Barber. Highly recommended. Contact www.cuf.org.

9. Catholic Scripture Study International's mission is "to bring people closer to Jesus Christ and His Church through in-depth Scripture study," www.cssprogram.net.

10. *Ignatius Press Study Bible* is available through www.ignatius.com. The entire New Testament should be released in one volume soon. Work is continuing on the Old Testament.

11. Schaeffer, p. 200.

12. See Gary Chapman, *The Five Love Languages: How to Express Heartfelt Commitment to Your Mate* (Chicago: Northfield, 1995). Dr. Chapman explains that there are five basic ways in which we naturally express love and interpret love, one of which is our primary love language.

CHAPTER EIGHT: *Waltzing Through Life: Establishing a Pattern to Our Tasks*

1. Holly Pierlot, *A Mother's Rule of Life: How to Bring Order to Your Home and Peace to Your Soul* (Manchester, N.H.: Sophia, 2004), p. 10.

2. See Paul J. Meyer, "Creating S.M.A.R.T. Goals," www.topachievement.com.

CHAPTER NINE: *A Mother's Guide to Confirmation*

1. Franz Delitzsch, *Biblical Commentary on the Prophecies of Isaiah,* Vol. 1 (Edinburgh: T & T Clark, 1869), p. 282.
2. Editorial staff at the Catholic University of America, *The New Catholic Encyclopedia*, Vol. 7 (New York: McGraw-Hill, 1967), p. 99.
3. *The New Catholic Encyclopedia*, vol. 7, p. 99.
4. *The New Catholic Encyclopedia*, vol. 7, p. 99.

PART FOUR: *She Provides Tasks for Her Maidens*

CHAPTER TEN: *Housework Is God's Work*

1. John Paul II, *Letter to Women*, no. 12, available at www.vatican.va.
2. *King James Version Bible.*
3. "Questions Without Answers," available at www.GCFL.net.
4. Pierlot, p. 11.
5. See Julie Morgenstern, *Organizing from the Inside Out: The Foolproof System for Organizing Your Home, Your Office and Your Life.* (New York: Henry Holt, 2004).
6. See Morgenstern, pp. 49–54.
7. Sandra Felton's organization, with more than ten thousand members, is called Messies Anonymous. The Web site address is www.messies.com.
8. Pam Young and Peggy Jones, *Sidetracked Home Executives: From Pigpen to Paradise*, Sydney Craft Rozen, ed. (New York: Warner, 1981), p. 35.
9. See Marla Cilley's new site, including products, www.housefairy.org; see www.thebratfactor.com.
10. James F. McElhone, *Particular Examen*, rev. ed. (Notre Dame, Ind.: Ave Maria, 1952), p. 73.
11. See *Chosen and Cherished*, chapter ten, "Conflict Resolution."

CHAPTER ELEVEN: *The Value of Homemaking*

1. Translation is from the *New American Bible*.
2. See *ADD-Friendly Ways to Organize Your Life* by Judith Kolberg, organization expert, and Dr. Kathleen Nadeau, psychologist and expert on ADD (New York: Brunner-Routledge, 2002).
3. Go to www.FlyLady.net.
4. Escrivá, p. 60, no. 185.
5. I cover this in more detail in the first book of this series, *Chosen and Cherished*.

PART FIVE: *She Considers a Field and Buys It*

CHAPTER THIRTEEN: *Good Management in the Garden of the Lord*

1. Dave Ramsey, *The Total Money Makeover: A Proven Plan for Financial Fitness* (Nashville: Nelson, 2007).

CHAPTER FOURTEEN: *Cultivating Contemplation*

1. *Hello Dolly!* script at www.script-o-rama.com.
2. Schaeffer, p. 86.
3. Go to www.gardensablaze.com for more information. For reading on companion gardens, see Sally Jean Cunningham, *Great Garden Companions: A Companion-Planting System for a Beautiful, Chemical-Free Vegetable Garden* (Emmaus, Pa.: Rodale, 1998).
4. See www.mgardens.org.
5. See www.fisheaters.com. *St. Anthony Messenger* magazine, published by St. Anthony Messenger Press, carried a feature article on Mary Gardens in its May 2000 issue, which can be accessed at www.americancatholic.org.
6. On June 28, 2005, I was privileged to witness Cardinal Ruini formally open the diocesan phase of John Paul II's cause for beatification. That is when "Servant of God" was attached to his name.

PART SIX: *She Girds Herself With Strength*

CHAPTER SIXTEEN: *Gird Your Loins With Strength*

1. "Understanding Women (A Man's Perspective)," found at www.darngoodfunnies.com.

CHAPTER EIGHTEEN: *A Mother's Guide to the Anointing of the Sick: Strength at the Hour of Death*

1. Michael Coniker's letter is quoted in Coniker, p. 202. The official cause for the canonization of Gwen Coniker was opened in June 2007. She is now referred to as Servant of God Gwen Coniker.

Life-Nurturing *Love*

building stronger, healthier marriages and families

GRACED AND GIFTED:
Book and DVD Boxed Set

Book #2 in the *Life-Nurturing Love* Series

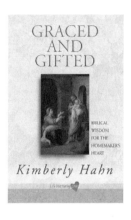

Graced and Gifted is also available as a boxed set with three DVDs. Containing Kimberly Hahn's lively and personable seminar presentation, this set is a valuable resource for small group discussion. The boxed set includes:

- the complete seminar manual
- *Graced and Gifted: Biblical Wisdom for the Homemaker's Heart*
- three DVDs (six complete sessions) of Hahn's presentation of the *Graced and Gifted* message to a seminar audience
- discussion questions to promote personal integration of the message into your life

Book and 3-DVD set
ISBN 978-0-86716-901-0
$59.99

Available from Servant Books, 1-800-488-0488,
www.ServantBooks.org

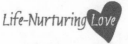

Life-Nurturing Love

building stronger, healthier marriages and families

Chosen and Cherished
Kimberly Hahn

Book #1 in the *Life-Nurturing Love* Series

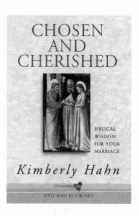

The first in a series of Bible studies based on Proverbs 31, *Chosen and Cherished* offers tools to help you build your marriage on the firm foundation of faith. Applying sacred Scripture, Church teaching and pastoral wisdom, Kimberly Hahn helps you explore:

- conflict resolution in your marriage
- communication skills with your spouse
- setting shared financial goals
- healing the wounds of unfaithfulness, and
- cultivating a spirit of generosity toward your spouse.

ISBN 978-0-86716-646-8 $14.99
Available from Servant Books, 1-800-488-0488,
www.ServantBooks.org

Chosen and Cherished is also available on a three DVD set, along with a copy of the book. This attractive boxed set includes Kimberly Hahn's lively presentation to a seminar audience. Discussion questions are included to help you apply the material to your own life. It is a valuable resource for small group discussion.

Book and 3-DVD set
ISBN 978-0-86716-859-4 $59.99
Available from Servant Books, 1-800-488-0488,
www.ServantBooks.org